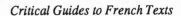
Critical Guides to French Texts

G000124335

90 Mauriac: Thérèse Desqueyroux

Critical Guides to French Texts

EDITED BY ROGER LITTLE, WOLFGANG VAN EMDEN, DAVID WILLIAMS

MAURIAC

Thérèse Desqueyroux

Toby Garfitt

Fellow and Tutor in French
Magdalen College, Oxford

Grant & Cutler Ltd
1991

ISBN 0 7293 0332 2

I.S.B.N. 84-599-3255-9

DEPÓSITO LEGAL: V. 2.845 - 1991

Printed in Spain by
Artes Gráficas Soler, S.A., Valencia
for
GRANT & CUTLER LTD
55-57 GREAT MARLBOROUGH STREET, LONDON W1V 2AY

Contents

References

All printings of the Livre de poche edition of *Thérèse Desqueyroux* up to and including that of 1988 (which has a six-page 'Postface' by François Mauriac's son Claude) have the same pagination for the text of the novel itself (pp.5-184). The 1989 edition by Jean Touzot is called a 'nouvelle édition revue et corrigée'. The text has been completely reset with a different pagination (pp.5-128), and it has also been slightly altered in places to follow that of the Pléiade or Fayard *Œuvres complètes*. For this reason, and to avoid confusion, references to the text of *Thérèse Desqueyroux* are here given in the form (p.47/63), where the first page number is that of the Touzot edition, and the second is that of the older Livre de poche editions. References to other works comprise an italicized number relating to the entry in the Bibliography, and a page number, thus: *42*, p.55.

1. Introduction

A reader encountering *Thérèse Desqueyroux* for the first time is likely to experience a sense of disorientation. In the first place, the title gives little away. It is evidently a woman's name, but the surname is strange to anyone who is not familiar with the south-west of France, and even its pronunciation presents difficulties.[1] Then, after an epigraph which suggests that the novel will be concerned with people who are in some way mad, or even monsters, there is a curious untitled page (which I shall refer to as the Foreword) in which Thérèse herself is addressed. This person is initially seen as a type rather than as an individual; and yet by the end of the Foreword she is apparently abandoned by the author on a pavement where he hopes she is not alone.

Things become a little clearer in the first chapter, which opens with Thérèse Desqueyroux leaving the court-house in a provincial town, a *sous-préfecture*, on a damp evening in autumn. Gradually the reader learns that she has been under investigation for the attempted poisoning of her husband, and that she is travelling home to meet him after the examining magistrate has decided that there is no case to answer. The geographical setting is established as the pine-forests of the Landes, but there is no indication of the exact date. The action may be roughly contemporary with the time of writing (the mid-1920s), but it could just as well take place before the First World War. Provincial society is seen as more or less static, although references to Bernard's Parisian education and to Jérôme Larroque's political careerism indicate the beginnings of change. There is no direct allusion to events in the outside world such as the

---

[1] The s is sounded. The middle syllable is pronounced locally as a diphthong (dɛskɛjru), but the pronunciation dɛskeru is the most commonly heard.

War, or to the political or economic situation of France. Furthermore, the text itself has a dreamy, introspective, quality which helps to create a sense of timelessness. Reading the novel is rather like stumbling through the dark, trying to identify landmarks which will make sense of the journey.

That of course, is what Thérèse herself is doing. Literally, because in the first nine chapters she is travelling home through the night, and metaphorically, because she is trying to work out how she came to administer poison to her husband. The reader is drawn into her train of thought, which develops beyond an attempt to prepare an explanation for Bernard into a search for herself, for an understanding of her own personality that will enable her to make sense of her past and to face up to it, as well as to her present and her future. The novel proves to be an exploration of an inner world, in which past, present and future are not in fact radically distinct from each other. Disorientation and lack of clarity, far from being obstacles to a proper understanding of the text, turn out to be essential to it.

There is plenty more to appreciate on the way, however, and the purpose of this guide is to make the reader's journey through the text an enriching experience. For that, it will be necessary to explore some areas whose importance may ultimately need reinterpretation. Thérèse does the same: she tries to account for her behaviour, examining a number of episodes from her past in the process, but has to accept that she remains a mystery to herself. So I shall analyse the characters of Bernard and others, for instance, although by the end of the novel it may seem that Thérèse herself is the only real character. In the same way I shall look at the social and geographical setting, even though Thérèse's inner world is what really matters. The reader of the novel is not in fact presented with an analysis of the social and economic dimensions of the society in which Thérèse lives, nor even with detailed descriptions of the landscape. The dampness of autumn and the torrid heat of summer affect Thérèse as much as do her social relationships, and the smell of the pine trees and the oppressiveness of their serried ranks are as significant as their economic importance. Nevertheless, a preliminary discussion of setting, themes and characters will at least provide points of entry into the novel, even if their relative importance has to be reassessed later.

2. Setting, Themes and Characters

The geographical setting of the novel is the south-eastern corner of the department of the Gironde, some fifty kilometres from Bordeaux. This area forms part of the large expanse of flat, sandy terrain, dotted with marshes and largely planted with pine-trees, which is known as the Landes. It is sometimes distinguished as 'la Lande girondine'. The administrative capital, the *sous-préfecture*, was until recently Bazas, referred to in the novel as B. (p.25/30), but it has now moved to Langon. A branch of the railway line from Bordeaux to the Mediterranean went off at Langon for Bazas and Mont-de-Marsan, and just before Bazas, at Le Nizan, there used to be another branch-line going via Uzeste and Villandraut to Saint-Symphorien (Saint-Clair in the novel).[2] Motor-cars were virtually unknown in the area even in the 1920s (Georges Franju's 1962 film of *Thérèse Desquey-roux*, in which Thérèse returns home not by train but by car, is clearly set much later), and distances seemed great.

Two generations or so earlier, during the Second Empire (1852-1870), the Landes had been planted with pines. People who had been shepherds in the marshes, getting about on stilts, now had the opportunity to become rich through the exploitation of the pines for resin (used to make turpentine) and for pit-props. They were now landowners, and their centre of existence moved to the small market-towns, where they occupied substantial stone-built houses, turning their original wooden family dwellings in the countryside over to tenant-farmers (*métayers*) who looked after the sheep and the pines on a share-cropping basis. The men would return to the *métairies* only to check on their property, or for the pigeon-shooting season in

---

[2]There is a well-known statue of Saint Clair at the church of Saint-Léger-de-Balson, 2 kilometres from Saint-Symphorien (the church used for Thérèse's wedding in the film).

the autumn, when they would be preoccupied with details of hides (*palombières*) and decoys (*appeaux*). For the rest of the year their conversation revolved around the pines: the price of resin, sales of timber, problems with tenants. In fact they remained very similar to the *métayers* in outlook and speech despite their social elevation. In the novel, even Bernard Desqueyroux, who has spent plenty of time away from home studying and travelling, still retains his 'manières frustes et sauvages' (p.26/33) and speaks patois. The impression of a closed culture, wrapped up in its own concerns and as difficult to break out of as it is for the reader or any outsider to penetrate, is emphasized by names such as Desqueyroux and La Téchoueyre and by regionalisms: 'brandes', 'fougasse', 'roumadjade', 'miques', or even 'quartier' in the special sense of a group of *métairies*.

Women play a full part in this society. Their place is clearly marked out. A woman has considerable status and responsibility, and it is inconceivable that such opportunities should be refused: she is not only mistress of a large house in the town, but is often the *de facto régisseuse* of a valuable estate, if her husband has a job which takes him away from home. He may not be up to it in any case: Thérèse comments that 'les femmes de la lande sont très supérieures aux hommes' (p.26/32). Thérèse herself is as passionately attached to her property, indeed to pine-plantations in general with the wealth that they represent, as any other member of her society. She is as careful as any man to stub out a cigarette before it can cause a disastrous fire, and she does so instinctively with her shoe even on a Paris pavement. She likes to talk property, pines and resin-yields with the men: 'les évaluations de propriétés la passionnaient' (p.31/40). Land and the family go together: a woman who raises a family is guaranteeing the continuity of ownership of the plantations. Her lot is therefore conventionally considered to be a happy one, with plenty to do looking after the family and the property. Even the winter, as 'le fils Deguilhem' puts it, 'n'est pas si terrible pour une femme qui aime son intérieur: "Il y a toujours tant de choses à faire dans une maison"' (p.115/164).

The major concern of such families is to maintain and consolidate their economic base, and to prepare the next generation to inherit it. If Bernard goes to study law in Paris, it is not with any intention of leaving his roots, but rather to enable him to run the family affairs more efficiently. Marriage is primarily a matter of property. Political differences, although sharp enough to cause family rows, are ultimately superficial in the eyes of 'ces personnes qui, de droite ou de gauche, n'en demeuraient pas moins d'accord sur ce principe essentiel: la propriété est l'unique bien de ce monde, et rien ne vaut de vivre que de posséder la terre' (p.59/80). Thérèse's father, Jérôme Larroque, is a radical in politics, and has his eye on a seat in the Senate. He is already a successful man. He has set up a factory in Saint-Clair to process resin and he has bought a sawmill in B., where he is now *maire* and a *conseiller général* for the department. Yet he is still keen to extend his base by a marriage alliance with the Desqueyroux family and their two thousand hectares of pines, despite their different political persuasion. The alliance suits Bernard too: his stepfather is not only virtually penniless, apart from some vineyards on the other side of the Garonne, but also spendthrift to the point of scandal, and there is every reason for Bernard to marry into a family whose wealth is secure. His marriage to Thérèse receives general approval: 'Tout le pays les mariait parce que leurs propriétés semblaient faites pour se confondre' (pp.25-26/31). These two powerful dynasties, who can summon up 'plus de cent métayers et domestiques' for the wedding (p.34/44), may differ both in politics and in religion, but they share an underlying caution and conservatism which make them clamp down on anything that might disturb the status quo. For all his anticlericalism and radicalism, Jérôme Larroque is concerned only to close ranks when a whiff of scandal might affect his own family. He does not even take his lawyer's advice to combat the rumour of his daughter's alleged crime in the local newspaper: he will use his influence with the *préfet* and with the press to make sure, on the contrary, that nothing is said, that the affair is simply hushed up.

Provincial society, then, is seen in the novel very much in terms of the family. Apart from the 'outsider' Jean Azévédo, all the principal characters belong to the two dynasties which come together in the marriage of Thérèse and Bernard: on her side, her father

Jérôme Larroque and her aunt Clara, and on Bernard's, his mother, Mme de La Trave, and his step-sister Anne.

Bernard Desqueyroux is an example of provincial society at its best. He possesses both wealth and intellect, and while he is as fond of hunting, eating and drinking as any of his peers, he is also a hard worker. He does not take his position for granted in respect of his family fortune, threatened by his stepfather's irresponsibility, or of his marriage. If he is to marry an educated woman, he accepts that 'un mari doit être plus instruit que sa femme' (p.26/32), and he has applied himself to his studies in Paris. He is efficient: 'il ne laissait rien au hasard et mettait son orgueil dans la bonne organisation de la vie' (p.26/31). His watchword is *régler*: 'Le pire des drames, voilà qu'il l'avait *réglé* comme n'importe quelle autre affaire' (p.93/129). He has even travelled, his trips to Italy, Spain and the Netherlands being, as one would expect, thoroughly planned in advance. In short, Bernard is 'très supérieur à son milieu' (p.60/81), and for Thérèse he is 'plus fin que la plupart des garçons' that she might have married (p.26/32).

It is this aspect of efficiency at organizing and manipulating that is mentioned first in the novel. In conversation with the lawyer Duros, Thérèse's father comments that 'après la déposition de mon gendre, c'était couru', and Duros echoes: 'La déposition de M. Desqueyroux était excellente, oui' (pp.9-11/8-9). On the other hand, Bernard is less good at coping with things that he does not understand. Thérèse notes that 'il ne parle guère de ce qu'il ne connaît pas; il accepte ses limites' (p.27/33). His area of competence is the land, with its pines and its birds and animals, and the family only in so far as it is associated with the land. When Thérèse is pregnant, he contemplates with respect 'la femme qui portait dans ses flancs le maître unique de pins sans nombre' (p.46-62). His interest in other people is functional: they must fit into his plans, or meet his needs. He likes to dominate, and he feels threatened by Thérèse's lack of straightforwardness: 'Il avait émis le vœu qu'elle devînt plus simple' (p.32/41). As an adolescent he was 'moins curieux des jeunes filles que du lièvre qu'il forçait dans la lande' (p.27/33). As an adult he conducts his sexual relationship with Thérèse like an animal (while she is reduced to the level of the inanimate, a thing that is there to be used and otherwise ignored): 'enfermé dans son plaisir comme ces jeunes porcs charmants qu'il est drôle de regarder à travers la grille, lorsqu'ils reniflent de bonheur dans une auge ("c'était moi, l'auge", songe Thérèse)' (p.35/46). At other times he is inclined to treat her like a captive bird or animal, and when he finally sets her free to go to Paris, Thérèse muses that it will be like the time he released a wild sow which he had been unable to tame (p.118/169).

A substantial figure in local society, then, and well integrated into the natural life of the Landes, Bernard's presence naturally pervades the text. In Chapter VII, for instance, the first word is 'Bernard', the first two pages emphasize his renewed vitality and assertiveness, and the final paragraph portrays him as a ruthless judge and gaoler. Luisa Borella suggests that 'cet éclairage circulaire, à peine en spirale, qui part du Bernard d'hier pour retourner au Bernard d'hier mais aussi au Bernard d'aujourd'hui' may imply that 'du haut de ses principes ... Bernard domine les personnalités tourmentées de Thérèse, Jean, Anne' (9, p.106). Yet for Thérèse he is curiously insubstantial. Her first references to him are as 'mon mari' and 'cet homme' (p.13/13) rather than by name. He is the one who is waiting for her, the one up against whom she will have to live, the one to whom she will make her confession, but not a person in his own right. In Chapter III she sketches a quick caricature of his life before their engagement, drawing on phrases used by himself and his mother, and categorizing him as 'ce garçon raisonnable' and 'ce jeune homme un peu trop gras' (p.26/31). She recognizes that there must be more to him: 'Sous la dure écorce de Bernard n'y avait-il pas une espèce de bonté? ... Oui, de la bonté, et aussi une justesse d'esprit, une grande bonne foi' (pp.26-27/33, cf. p.64/89). But she does not explore any further, and indeed Bernard fades before the memory of his sister Anne. Thérèse's subsequent attempt to explain why she married him suggests that his personality was relatively unimportant. She was attracted by his pines and by the security, the 'refuge', afforded by marriage. Bernard himself is seen as a stranger, a member of 'la race implacable des simples' with little in common with her 'monde confus' (p.30/38). It is remarkable that the brief account of the wedding at the beginning of Chapter IV contains not a single direct reference to Bernard, either by name or as the bride-groom. Even the paragraph devoted to the wedding night and the beginning of the honeymoon mentions him only as 'un mari' and 'un homme': the depersonalization continues later in the chapter with references to 'cet homme' and 'Adam'. In Chapter IX, when Thérèse at last reaches Argelouse and meets Bernard, he is still referred to as 'cet homme' (p.88/123). He is presented, indeed he presents himself, as the spokesman of the family: 'Vous obéirez aux décisions arrêtées en famille, sinon ... Moi, je m'efface: la famille compte seule. L'intérêt de la famille a toujours dicté toutes mes décisions' (pp.90-91/125-26, cf. p.73/100). In his last speech in the novel he again defines himself in terms of the continuing dynasty: 'Chaque généra-tion de Desqueyroux a eu son vieux garçon! Il fallait bien que ce fût moi' (p.126/182). The whole episode of his marriage to Thérèse has been just a moment in the history of his race.

On a recent adult education course in Bordeaux, while ten of the fifteen participants found Thérèse to be 'le personnage qui vous a le plus touché' in the novel, three chose Bernard (all men), and two chose Anne (27, p.121). Anne de La Trave used to fascinate Thérèse as a child. She is first mentioned in the novel as 'sa dévote amie', 'petite sœur Anne, chère innocente' (p.18/21), associated with religious purity, in contrast to Thérèse, the 'lycéenne raisonneuse et moqueuse' whose upbringing had been atheistic. The two were inseparable in the school holidays. Thérèse preserves an image of them 'se tenant par la taille' with their 'longues ombres confondues' on the moonlit road (p.20/23). She senses that if she is going to explain anything to Bernard, she must begin by talking about Anne. Indeed, when she tries to think about her husband, it is Anne whose picture surges into her mind instead (p.27/33). Anne is no ethereal being despite her aura of spirituality. It is her body that Thérèse remembers: 'le visage en feu', 'sa bouche minuscule', 'les genoux rapprochés', 'ses lèvres' (pp.27-29/33-36). Her mind, on the other hand, was empty: 'Elle haïssait la lecture, n'aimait que coudre, jacasser et rire. Aucune idée sur rien' (pp.27-28/34, cf. pp.49/65-66). In the manuscript Mauriac had emphasized the physical aspect even more strongly: 'Rien de mystérieux dans cette petite fille SINON SON CORPS' (with a double underlining, and a note in the margin: 'insister') (2, p.945). Even without that indication it is clear that Thérèse was to some extent uneasy about her attraction to Anne. When they were lying looking up at the sky, she remembers that: 'avant que Thérèse ait eu le temps de distinguer la femme ailée qu'Anne voyait dans le ciel, ce n'était déjà plus, disait la jeune fille, qu'une étrange bête étendue' (p.28/35). The implication is that a pure relationship could also be seen as something physical, animal and ugly. Critics have not surprisingly interpreted the attachment as at least potentially a homosexual one, and Georges Franju has been criticized for overemphasizing that aspect in his film (*34*, p.151). It has been pointed out that by marrying Anne's step-brother, Thérèse is in a sense marrying her (p.31/39; *39*, p.138; *36*, p.26). That may be part of it, but on another level Anne and Thérèse can be seen as two complementary facets of the same character. Anne will later represent an alternative, and more orthodox, model of a woman in this particular society, but to begin with she forms with Thérèse a kind of dual being, as shown by their 'ombres confondues'. Anne is associated with the full moon and the sun ('son amie ... la voyait au milieu du seigle viser le soleil comme pour l'éteindre', p.29/36), while Thérèse seems to belong to darkness and night (but see *38*). Mauriac often portrays similar pairs. In his next novel, *Destins*, Bob and Pierre are the same age, one attractive, superficial and socially successful, and the other unprepossessing, earnest and religious. Their destinies are closely intertwined. In the novel after that, *Ce qui était perdu*, Alain Forcas and his sister appear almost as two contrasting but complementary manifestations of a single hermaphroditic being.

One of Anne's major functions is to awaken latent possibilities in Thérèse. When she goes out shooting larks, Thérèse, who 'haïssait ce jeu', watches her hold the wounded bird in her hands and stifle it, 'tout en caressant de ses lèvres les plumes chaudes' (p.29/36). Thérèse will later act destructively towards those who are close to her: Anne, Bernard, her own daughter Marie (over whom she stoops with a similarly ambiguous gesture: 'ses lèvres chercheront, comme de l'eau, cette vie endormie', p.12/11) and of course herself. But it is in her passionate affair with Jean Azévédo that Anne has the most dramatic effect on Thérèse,[3] significantly in the middle of the latter's honeymoon. It is when she ceases to be a 'fantôme' (p.41/56) and becomes the real Anne whom Thérèse never knew, enjoying a real relationship of passion (or so it appears), that she arouses Thérèse's jealousy and destructiveness. In so doing she also opens up the way for the illumination that Thérèse will herself receive from Jean. It is Anne who pushes Thérèse into the role of 'une femme de la famille' (p.72/99), a woman who accepts her place and is imbued with 'l'esprit de famille'. In fact this is a false role: in terms of social and family expectations Thérèse is only a 'pseudo-épouse' and 'pseudo-mère' (see *29*), and it will not be long before the true 'femme de la famille' is revealed to be not her but Anne. Anne acts in practice as the mother of Thérèse's child (pp.78-79/109), and Thérèse later reflects that Anne 'n'attend que d'avoir des enfants pour s'anéantir en eux, comme a fait sa mère, comme font toutes les femmes de la famille' (p.115/165).

Thérèse longed to be with Anne when they were children, but was sometimes rebuffed (e.g. pp.29/36-37). During Anne's affair with Jean Azévédo, Thérèse is both supportive and destructive towards her. There are powerful emotional bonds between them, and it could be argued that the couple Anne-Thérèse is at the centre of the novel in a way that the couple Thérèse-Bernard is not (see *36*, p.25).

Anne's mother, Mme de La Trave, is perhaps the most powerful figure in the novel apart from Thérèse herself. She is the archetypal 'femme de la famille', exercising matriarchal authority: not as dominant and destructive as Félicité Cazenave in *Genitrix*, but cast in the same mould. Her imperious nature, combined with the weakness of her husband, may help to explain 'le caractère soumis de Bernard, son enserrement dans des valeurs matricielles, son incapacité d'être homme et sa résignation' (*39*, pp.137-38). She appears as the voice of the family, justifying Bernard's marriage to

---

[3] 'Tous les dialogues qui ont une certaine longueur concernent la liaison d'Anne et de Jean' (*17*, p.21).

Thérèse despite the social obstacles (her smoking, the scandal of her grandmother, and her father's anticlericalism and radicalism; but of course Jérôme Larroque is rich and influential, and Thérèse adores Bernard) (pp.30/38-39). She is someone who organizes and defines, labelling Thérèse, despite her lifestyle, as 'une nature très droite, franche comme l'or' (p.30/38), and her father as 'un saint laïque' (p.30/39). But above all, she is the one who organizes the imprisonment of her own daughter in order to make her break off the affair with Jean Azévédo and accept a dynastic marriage to 'le fils Deguilhem'. Although the chapter which deals with that episode begins with three references to 'le couple La Trave' or 'les La Trave', it is clear before the end of the first paragraph that she is the driving force. Her authoritative clichés override the timid compromises of her husband.[4]

Mme de La Trave has a remedy for every problem. When Anne will not eat, she declares that 'on se force' (p.51/70). When Thérèse cannot face the spectacle of Bernard eating, her mother-in-law puts it down to her pregnancy, and recalls that when she herself was pregnant she had to 'respirer une balle de caoutchouc: il n'y avait que ça pour me remettre l'estomac en place' (p.52/70). People are treated not as individuals with particular needs, but in terms of a community which operates according to unquestioned principles. Thérèse realizes that 'les La Trave vénéraient en moi un vase sacré; le réceptacle de leur progéniture; aucun doute que, le cas échéant, ils m'eussent sacrifiée à cet embryon' (p.75/104). Anything that does not fit the accepted pattern must be either explained away or else rejected. To begin with, at any rate, Thérèse falls into the first category: if she shows no interest in getting the baby's layette ready, it is because 'ce n'était pas sa partie' (p.75/103), and after the birth, if 'ce n'est pas dans ses cordes' to attend to the practical details,

---

[4] M. de La Trave, whose name changes from Victor (p.25/31) to Hector (p.48/64) (exactly the same as happens in the case of M. Larousselle in *Le Désert de l'amour*), may be a weak spendthrift (p.25/31), but he is one of the few characters to show any compassion. He also keeps alive the theme of the 'voyage d'amour' (p.49/66), of which Thérèse's honeymoon had been such a caricature.

nevertheless 'Mme de La Trave assurait qu'elle aimait sa fille à sa manière' (p.78/108). The young priest, on the other hand, is quickly dismissed: he may be punctilious about services, and studious too, but he neglects the parish, and 'ce n'est pas le genre qu'il faut ici' (p.76/105: the verdict, although unattributed, sounds like hers). Having expressed surprise at Thérèse's sudden churchgoing ('Vous vous y décidez, ma petite, juste au moment où votre état vous en aurait dispensée'), it is probably also Mme de La Trave who discourages her from attending weekday services as well: 'cette démarche eût paru étrange à sa famille et aux gens du bourg, on aurait crié à la conversion' (pp.77/106-07).

Even more than Bernard, then, it is Mme de La Trave who represents the rigid orthodoxy of the family. Revolt must be suppressed either linguistically or physically, and it is she who assumes the task of convincing the rest of society that there is nothing the matter. Not only does she stand next to Thérèse in church to demonstrate the solidarity of the family, but she represents her as an innocent victim: 'Nous craignons que la pauvre petite ne s'en relève pas; elle ne veut voir personne et le médecin dit qu'il ne faut pas la contrarier, Bernard l'entoure beaucoup, mais le moral est atteint' (p.102/145). Yet paradoxically Mme de La Trave holds the key not only to the society which she embodies but also to the alternative world inhabited by Thérèse. Her last recorded words are 'elle fait semblant' (p.117/167): in order to survive, everyone must 'faire semblant', and she is more conscious of that than any other character in the novel. In this respect she acts as an authorial mouthpiece. If she defines Thérèse's attitude to the family as 'hypocrisie' (p.113/161), that value judgment can obviously rebound on herself and on the whole of provincial society. Conversely — and herein lies the paradox — she shows a remarkable ability to validate what does not at first sight appear to conform to expectations. I have already mentioned her explanations of Thérèse's unorthodox behaviour. An even more striking example is her detailed commentary on Anne's hat, which may look plain and ordinary, but which she claims to be something special (pp.112/160-61). If Bernard and Jérôme Larroque respond to nonconformity by stifling it, Mme de La Trave on the contrary emphasizes the gulf betweeen appearance and reality, thus drawing attention to the possibility that Thérèse may after all be at least as authentic and precious as the unprepossessing hat. It is in the character of Mme de La Trave, then, that the values of provincial society find their potential subversion as well as their most pungently formulaic expression.

Jérôme Larroque's mixture of social conservatism and political ambition has already been mentioned. He might be expected to be a powerful figure in the novel as he clearly is in society, but in fact he is portrayed as weak. Although he owns a factory in Saint-Clair his home is at B.: the pines came to him from his wife, and he does not really belong. We are first introduced to him as someone who is scarcely human: 'Un homme, dont le col était relevé, se détacha d'un platane; elle reconnut son père ... Son père ne l'embrassa pas, ne lui donna pas même un regard' (p.9/7). His body is caricaturally small ('petit homme aux courtes jambes arquées', p.10/9). The important feature is his voice: a falsetto voice, given to a kind of incantatory repetition:

> Mais malheureuse, trouve autre chose ... trouve autre
> chose ... (p.11/10, cf. p.84/118);
>
> Il faut recouvrir tout ça ... il faut recouvrir ... (p.11/11);
>
> Il faut que vous soyez comme les deux doigts de
> la main ... comme les deux doigts de la main, entends-
> tu? (p.15/16)

Thérèse is an obstacle to him, not only socially and politically (p.13/13), but physically as well: 'gênés par ce corps de femme qui les séparait' (p.10/9). Indeed all women are an embarrassment. His 'mépris des femmes' (p.58/79) manifests itself in his habitual description of them as 'toutes des hystériques quand elles ne sont pas des idiotes' (pp.13, 58/13, 79) and in his general prudishness: he never had a mistress either before his marriage or after his wife's death, and certain topics of conversation make him blush 'comme un adolescent' (p.58/79). He is socially repressive too. It is he who first utters the word 'étouffement' (p.11/10) and guarantees to stifle the scandal about Thérèse. He must preserve the status quo, even refusing to 'rien changer à ce domaine d'Argelouse' (p.25/30) since the death of his wife.

For Thérèse, her father is significant not only as the symbol of repression but also for what he fails to embody. She has tried to see him as the representative of authority, worthy of respect: 'Le seul homme supérieur qu'elle crût connaître, c'était son père. Elle s'efforçait de prêter quelque grandeur à ce radical entêté, méfiant' (p.58/78). When arguments about religion arise with her in-laws, 'elle se précipitait au secours de M. Larroque' (p.59/78). But she is unable to shore him up, to give him the rock-like quality of which his name ironically speaks. She is obliged to look elsewhere, to the 'bloc familial' (p.31/40) afforded by marriage, to Jean Azévédo, to a magistrate whom she sees in her dream, omniscient unlike the one who dismissed her case (p.17/20), and perhaps to a dimly-perceived God. Jérôme Larroque virtually disappears from the text early on, the last of a series of parental figures who have failed Thérèse (but while her mother and grandmother may fail her simply through absence, the latter, at least, offers her an inspiring model of nonconformity).

His sister, Thérèse's aunt Clara, has a more positive role to play. She is first introduced as a substitute mother-figure, inhabiting the mother's house at Argelouse, and welcoming Thérèse during the holidays. Being stone deaf, she is identified with nature rather than with humans: she liked the solitude of the forest because 'elle n'y voyait pas, disait-elle, les lèvres des autres remuer' and because 'on n'y pouvait rien entendre que le vent dans les pins' (p.25/30). On her next appearance she is associated with Thérèse's idyllic friendship with Anne, but even more important than that is the parallel that is established with Thérèse herself: 'Le silence n'était pas plus profond pour la sourde immobile et les mains croisées sur la nappe, que pour cette jeune fille un peu hagarde' (p.30/38). Later she will be characterized as an 'emmurée vivante' (p.88/122). She is thus presented as a possible model for Thérèse, still a part of the family, unlike the disgraced grandmother, and yet living a life of her own in communion with nature, more authentic in both her faith and her

revolt than the rest of them (p.59/80). Ironically, Thérèse is no less
guilty than anyone else of rejecting Clara: 'ce fut toujours sa
malchance d'entrer chez Thérèse au moment où la jeune femme
souhaitait d'être seule. Souvent, il avait suffi à la vieille d'entrouvrir
la porte, pour se sentir importune' (p.95/133). I shall discuss the
significance of Clara's name and of her death later. For the moment
she can be seen as embodying some of the contradictions that
Thérèse herself experiences, and offering a possible, though not
entirely satisfactory, resolution.

The last major character to consider, apart from Thérèse
herself, is Jean Azévédo. It is perhaps surprising to find references to
him in eleven of the thirteen chapters of the novel. He seems initially
to be only an episodic character, a friend of a friend of Thérèse. Yet
his brief acquaintance with Thérèse establishes him as a central
figure in her search for identity and meaning. He enables her to see
her family and society for what they are. He formulates the striking
image of 'cette immense et uniforme surface de gel où toutes les
âmes ici sont prises; parfois une crevasse découvre l'eau noire:
quelqu'un s'est débattu, a disparu; la croûte se reforme' (p.68/93), and
provokes in her mind the no less striking image of the cart that is
'à la voie', always following the same ruts (p.65/89). He reawakens
in her the love of books which she had as a child, and suggests new
avenues to explore, those of individualistic philosophy and
mysticism. He also comes to represent Paris for her, so that her
dreams of a new life there involve her going 'droit chez Jean
Azévédo' (p.106/150).

Jean is defined first in terms of family, health and place: he is
'le fils Azévédo', a tubercular patient who has come to live at
Vilméja (pp.36, 37/47, 49). On all those counts he is a threat. The
son of a Bordeaux family, said to be of Portuguese Jewish origin,
and tainted with illness, he represents the archetypal dangerous
outsider for the closed society of the Landes. What is more, it was to
Vilméja that Thérèse and Bernard used to walk when they were
courting (p.32/41), and Anne complains that she can no longer 'aller
du côté de Vilméja' since his arrival (p.36/47). To those who are
adventurous enough to cross the social barriers, Jean Azévédo

reveals the unknown: emotional, social and intellectual liberation. According to Georges Mounin, his significance for Thérèse is that he provides her with 'les justifications qui lui permettent ... de s'accepter, de devenir ce qu'elle est' (*36*, p.30). His doctrine is a mixture of Nietzsche, Barrès and Gide (*25*, p.130), calculated to appeal to this 'lycéenne raisonneuse et moqueuse' (p.18/22), heir of 'the Rousseauist dechristianisation of moral analysis' (*44*, p.52), whose 'conscience est son unique et suffisante lumière' (p.21/26). Malcolm Scott has pointed out that 'Azévédo expresses the preoccupations which run through Gide's writings, but they are stripped of the irony which is the vehicle of Gide's moral caution, and thus they embody that vulgarisation and distortion of Gide's ideas that was prevalent in the post-war generation' (*44*, p.49). The individualism preached by Jean is superficially attractive, like that of the Parisian intellectual set whom Mauriac found both fascinating and shallow. Shortly after completing *Thérèse Desqueyroux*, Mauriac was to be faced with reconciling the intellectual and artistic doctrines of Gidism, on the one hand, with his own deeply-held moral and religious views, on the other (see below, p.33).

While the ideas expressed by Jean Azévédo are therefore important both for Thérèse and for Mauriac himself, the character of Jean has little substance. Other characters project on to him their own deep fears and desires. Alternatively he can be seen as a mirror in which they see themselves and their situation in a new light. When Thérèse looked at the photograph of Jean that Anne had sent, she 'reconnut l'endroit', and immediately afterwards she 'leva les yeux et fut étonnée de sa figure dans la glace' (p.40/53). Jean's relationships with Anne and then with Thérèse, or rather theirs with him, are important in the novel, but he never acquires any depth.

It will have become clear that there is an element of social satire in *Thérèse Desqueyroux*, as in all of Mauriac's novels. Indeed, he had originally planned to call it *L'Esprit de famille*, with as its major theme the propensity of the provincial family to stifle scandal at all costs (see *2*, p.929). Mauriac noted that the secret sub-title was to be 'le plat de cendre', the litter-tray in which a household pet covers up its mess: that is the connotation of Jérôme Larroque's remark that 'pour la famille, il faut recouvrir tout ça' (p.11/11). There are in fact three scandals which are stifled in the novel: not only that of Thérèse, but those involving her grandmother Julie Bellade, who was obliterated from the family record, and Anne, whose unsuitable affair with Jean is suppressed with Thérèse's help. Of course the idea of 'étouffement' has grown and evolved beyond the mere stifling of scandal, becoming integral to Thérèse's whole personality and not simply characteristic of the behaviour of society, but that aspect is still important. *Thérèse Desqueyroux* is still, on one level, a stinging indictment of the provincial society of Mauriac's childhood, with at its centre the family, obsessed with property and respectability, and characterized by hypocrisy.

The picture of provincial society is filled out by several minor characters, each of whom is neatly defined in terms both of social position and of personality. There is Duros the lawyer who likes to have his finger in every pie; Gardère the coachman with the devouring stare; the family retainers Balion and Balionte (the latter not only acting as Thérèse's gaoler but also taking on Clara's role of providing a mixture of sympathy and provocation); Pédemay the local doctor, concerned with his own reputation as much as with the health of his patient; and 'le fils Deguilhem', never favoured with a Christian name, chosen by the family as an appropriate match for Anne, with his bald head, his drooping shoulders, his 'petites cuisses grasses sous un pantalon rayé gris et noir' (p.114/164), and his predictable conversation. It is significant that they each find it hard to come to terms with Thérèse. Thérèse is the one character who has not yet been examined, and we must look again at the themes that have been mentioned in connection with the family and society — property, hypocrisy, the place of women, sexuality, repression, religion, self-knowledge, etc. — in relation to her.

It is, of course, possible to see Thérèse as the focus of revolt against the repressive environment. We first meet her at the end of a long judicial investigation into a serious crime against the family. Her father virtually disowns her. Her isolation is emphasized: in the town, in the *calèche* where she realizes that she is 'condamnée à la solitude éternelle' (p.17/19), in the train, in the *carriole* which she

sees as a last 'refuge' (p.86/119) ... and at Argelouse. During the
journey, as she remembers her past life, plenty of evidence of
subversiveness comes to light. At school, although her teachers held
her up as an example, she was aware of failing to fit into their
categories. At the same time, by virtue of the very qualities that they
extolled in her ('cette joie de réaliser en elle un type d'humanité
supérieure', 'l'orgueil d'appartenir à l'élite humaine', p.21/26), as well
as her intellect, she was setting herself apart from a society in which
conformity and practical skills were what was expected of women.
The influence of her father combined with that of the *lycée* helped to
make her 'raisonneuse et moqueuse' (p.18/22), critical of the
respectability of families like the La Traves. Her smoking is no
doubt a deliberate act of defiance: as Mme de La Trave says, it is 'un
genre qu'elle se donne', copied from unconventional and probably
loose women of the world who do not share the 'principes' and 'idées
saines' of respectable society (p.30/38). In this society whose liveli-
hood depends on pine-trees, Thérèse dreams of being the metaphorical spark that sets off a destructive forest fire (p.33/43), and later of
starting a real fire (p.80/111). Once trapped in a dynastic marriage,
she rejects the part of a 'femme de la famille': she champions her
own individuality and refuses to live simply for the child that she
bears. She associates with two people whom her society holds at
arm's length, Jean Azévédo and the young parish priest. Both
reinforce her feeling that her society is narrow and petty, and
encourage a subversive quest for something more authentic, more
spiritual. Her revolt finds an opportunity in Bernard's mistake about
his medicine: by undermining the health of the husband, the head of
the family, the proprietor, she can assert herself as a free woman.
Her suicide attempt is also an act of revolt. Death by suicide would
be not only a release from society, but also an affront to bourgeois
Christian principles. During her imprisonment at Argelouse she
settles for a policy of passive resistance, and after a war of attrition
she finally wins her freedom. Paris offers her the chance to be
herself, to create a new, authentic life which will be under her own
control.

There is clearly some truth in such a view. Mauriac himself commented in an interview that *Thérèse Desqueyroux* was 'le roman de la révolte' (quoted by Jenkins, p.29), and Thérèse herself is the only character who can embody that revolt to any convincing extent. Anne's rebellion is short-lived, and Jean Azévédo, while showing up provincial society, is not himself portrayed as a rebel against his own environment. Yet Thérèse's revolt, real as it is, is only partial, and in any case it is the expression of only one aspect of her personality. It is partial, because she is at the same time deeply committed to the values of her society. Her attitude to property is no different from that of her family. In her fantasy about starting a forest fire it is stated that she has 'l'amour des pins dans le sang', and that 'ce n'était pas aux arbres qu'allait sa haine' (p.80/111). What is more, her marriage was not purely a dynastic affair. She wanted the security and status that it would bring. She may have been motivated by panic, but she was happy to find the 'refuge' and 'ordre' of the 'bloc familial' (p.31/40). She was not rebelling against the family and society at that point. Indeed, in the campaign against Anne's affair with Jean Azévédo, Thérèse acts as an agent of the family, calling forth from Anne the reproach of hypocrisy (p.72 / 99). As for the poisoning of Bernard, if that were truly an act of revolt, Thérèse would surely be proud to acknowledge herself as a criminal in the eyes of society: yet she is unable to see it as a crime. 'Moi, je ne connais pas mes crimes. Je n'ai pas voulu celui dont on me charge' (p.19/22). When she finally reaches Paris, she is filled with nostalgia for Argelouse — from which she has never actually run away, unlike her grandmother Julie Bellade, or the murderer Daguerre whose flight she thinks of emulating (p.97/136). She will also continue to be dependent on Bernard to look after her financial affairs.

The attempt to classify Thérèse as a rebel has therefore not been wholly successful, although she does undoubtedly call her society into question, and perhaps ours too (particularly in the exploration of her womanhood). It will have become clear by now that *Thérèse Desqueyroux* is far more than a social document or even a social satire. Before proceeding any further, it may be helpful to look at the genesis of the novel.

3. Mauriac's Starting Points

Mauriac and the Novel in 1926-27

On 4 February 1927, a few days before the publication of *Thérèse Desqueyroux* in book form (it had already appeared in instalments in *La Revue de Paris* between 15 November 1926 and 1 January 1927), Mauriac gave a lecture to the Société des Conférences. The lecture, together with an article which had appeared in *Les Nouvelles littéraires* on 8 January, was later published under the title *Le Roman*. It provides useful insights into Mauriac's understanding of the novel as a genre, and of his own current practice in particular.

First of all, Mauriac is at pains to distinguish the novel proper from 'des essais, des notes de voyage, des impressions déguisées en récits romanesques' (2, p.1331). 'Pour avoir le droit de se dire romancier, il faut pouvoir donner la vie, il faut créer des êtres vivants' (2, p.1332). That means, for him, choosing a provincial setting. In an earlier essay entitled *La Province* (1926), he had already argued that Paris is out of touch with the rhythms of the natural world, and is also characterless, simply because everything is possible. In the provinces, on the other hand, particularly before the War, the social structures left very little possibility of manœuvre. As a result, 'contenue par les barrages de la religion, par les hiérarchies sociales, la passion s'accumule dans les cœurs' (2, p.726). The Landes, where Mauriac, brought up in Bordeaux, used to spend his school holidays (a further explanation for the impression that is given in *Thérèse Desqueyroux* of a world where time stopped in about 1900), provided him with an example of a tightly-structured environment — both refuge and prison — which was an ideal setting for novels of passion. For the novelist, he concluded, 'l'unique nécessaire n'est donc pas de vivre à Paris, mais d'avoir longtemps vécu, lutté, souffert au plus secret d'une province' (2, p.746). Taking up a point from *La Province*, Mauriac now comments that

> Il arrive souvent que le jeune homme, aujourd'hui, n'accepte d'entrer en conflit ni avec une religion à laquelle il n'adhère pas, ni avec une morale issue de cette religion, ni avec un honneur mondain issu de cette morale. (2, p.752)

He defines the modern age as one in which 'ce qui touche à la chair a perdu toute importance' (2, p.753), that is to say, where human relationships are no longer problematical. Love is no longer hemmed about by customs, taboos and expectations. It has lost all its mystery, and the novel is the poorer for it. One solution has been to explore in more detail than before the physical aspects of human sexuality.

> Le romancier se trouve donc amené à ne plus s'attacher à d'autres sujets que la chair. Les autres régions lui étant interdites, le romancier s'aventure, avec une audace croissante, sur des terres maudites où naguère encore nul n'aurait osé s'engager. (2, p.757)

Mauriac instances Gide, Proust, Joyce, Colette and others, and adds: 'et je prêche un peu pour ma paroisse'.

Hand in hand with this new boldness goes an impatience with the nineteenth-century tradition of considering the individual primarily in terms of a social group. Proust and Gide, in particular, have led the way in exploring the distinctiveness of each individual person, however superficially normal, and discovering in each 'le plus irremplaçable des êtres' (Gide's phrase), which Mauriac glosses as 'à la lettre, un monstre' (2, p.762). Thanks to Dostoevsky, apparently illogical and contradictory characters have superseded the logical constructions of Balzac and the French tradition in general, leaving the French novelist in a dilemma.

Il s'agit de laisser à nos héros l'illogisme, l'indéter-
mination, la complexité des êtres vivants; et tout de
même de continuer à construire, à ordonner, selon le
génie de notre race, — de demeurer enfin des écrivains
d'ordre et de clarté. (2, p.756)

Mauriac sums up the dual aspiration of the modern French novelist
as: 'Tout oser dire, mais tout oser dire chastement' (2, p.766).

In passing, he has noted that such a programme presents a
problem to the Christian. Jacques Maritain, the Catholic philosopher,
had condemned this 'regard jeté sur les plus secrets mystères de la
sensibilité' (2, p.757) as no better than voyeurism: only God has the
right to sound the depths of the human heart. That is perhaps one
reason why Mauriac assimilates the novelist to God (in the published
version, the essay begins with the resounding statement that: 'Le
romancier est, de tous les hommes, celui qui ressemble le plus à
Dieu', 2, p.751). The relationship between the author and his
characters is obviously extremely delicate, and Mauriac sees it in
terms of a balance between the theological concepts of free will and
predestination. The novelist creates his characters, but also allows
them a life of their own. Mauriac's own preference is for 'l'enfant
récalcitrant, l'enfant prodigue' rather than 'l'enfant sage': characters
who do not behave entirely as expected give him the sense of 'le
battement même du cœur de chair que nous leur avons donné' (2,
p.767). In order to maintain the balance, he argues that the novelist
cannot respect 'le secret des cœurs': rather, his duty, his vocation, is
to violate it. At the same time, he must do full justice to the systems
of morality, ideology, faith and so on to which people do in fact sub-
scribe and by which, on the whole, they run their lives. If Proust had
a weakness as a novelist it was a 'défaut de perspective morale' (2,
p.770), a failure to portray the workings of conscience. In the article
appended to the essay Mauriac completes his reply to Maritain by
arguing that there must be a genuine 'connivence' between the
novelist and his corrupt characters, that the author cannot be a saint
or he would not write novels. That does not stop him from having
faith that a true depiction of what people are really like inside is the

best pointer to their need of divine grace. In that sense the novel
portrays what Pascal called 'la misère de l'homme sans Dieu'.

Mauriac, then, sees himself as a modern novelist in the line of
Gide and the others he mentions, using the insights of Dostoevsky
and no doubt Freud (whom he only mentions by name in a quotation
from Maritain) to probe the mysterious depths of individual personality, but without abandoning the French classical tradition of *pudeur*
or a Christian understanding of the world. He accepts that the most
apparently normal human being will tend to be portrayed as a
'monstre', a word which echoes not only the epigraph and Foreword
of *Thérèse Desqueyroux* but Thérèse's own self-assessment. His
brief is to explore emotion, including sexuality, while reintroducing
into the modern novel the restrictions which society used to place
around relationships, and which have remained intact in the
provincial world of his fiction. He will create characters with a
proper social and ideological context, but he will engage in a
dynamic relationship with them, accepting that he cannot fully
control them.

That provides a helpful summary of what Mauriac feels he has
just achieved in *Thérèse Desqueyroux*. It is a useful corrective to his
later definition of it as 'le roman de la révolte'. While a satirical
attack on the hypocrisy and stifling atmosphere of provincial society
was clearly a major part of his original intention in writing the novel,
Mauriac now recognizes, having completed it, that that was only the
necessary context for something else: the exploration of the inner
world of a single character, with all its dark corners and contradictions. He also recognizes his lack of control over that character: far
from being a mere vehicle for his criticisms of society, Thérèse has
taken on a life of her own, and Mauriac may already be aware that
he has not finished with her yet.

Mauriac and Thérèse

It is a truism that a novelist will base his main characters on aspects
of his own personality. Of course many of the details will be derived
from other models, mythical, literary or observed, but the inner life

must be fuelled by the writer's self-knowledge. Mauriac seems to have been obsessed by the figure of Thérèse over a period of about ten years, and the obvious implication is that she represented an essential part of his own personality, at a time when he was struggling to come to terms with himself.

In *Thérèse Desqueyroux*, in which she makes her first appearance, Mauriac treats her as a real person, addressing her directly in the Foreword and several times in the body of the novel too, and expressing the hope that she will conquer her solitude and discover a companionship which, for him at least, has religious overtones. A year after the publication of that novel he sketched out a page which was to be part of a projected *Fin de Thérèse* (see *3*, pp.976-77). In *Ce qui était perdu*, begun in 1929 and published in 1930, he not only created another remarkable intellectual woman, Irène de Blénauge, who has been shown to be 'une variation possible de Thérèse qui reste le personnage dominant' (*47*, p.117), but he allowed Thérèse herself to invade the text. In a striking episode, one of the protagonists encounters Thérèse on a bench in Paris after the break-up of her relationship with Jean Azévédo (*2*, pp.311-13). Then in 1932 and 1933 Mauriac wrote two short stories, *Thérèse chez le docteur* and *Thérèse à l'hôtel*, before making Thérèse the main character in a second novel, *La Fin de la nuit*, published in 1935. The character naturally evolves over this period. I shall be concerned only with the Thérèse of the original novel, but it is at least clear that Mauriac felt that he was dealing with someone who exercised a real fascination over him.

It is not quite accurate to say that Thérèse Desqueyroux makes her first appearance in the novel which bears her name. There exists a short first draft entitled *Conscience, instinct divin* (see *2*, pp.1-13). It is in the form of a written confession to a priest, in which an unnamed young woman admits to having tried to poison her otherwise quite satisfactory husband because she cannot cope with his sexual demands: indeed, she sees murder as a charitable act of deliverance, delivering *him* from his base carnal nature. Several of Mauriac's previous novels had begun their existence in a similar confessional form, notably *Le Baiser au lépreux* (1922). Here, however, it is not simply a conventional first-person narrative form, but a specific confession of guilt, to a priest. The figure of Thérèse seems to have crystallized around the ideas of an abhorrence of the sexual act, murder, and confession.

Guilt and the fear of sex had been very much part of Mauriac's childhood. He was brought up by a pious, widowed mother in a highly religious and morally scrupulous atmosphere which could have been that of the seventeenth century. In his *Vie de Jean Racine*, written in 1927 and published in 1928, Mauriac evokes Racine's childhood in terms which show that he is drawing on his own memories:

> Un esprit chrétien rigoureux y règle les moindres gestes
> de la vie quotidienne. Nous savons ce que c'est que de
> vivre, dès ses premières années, dans une sorte de terreur
> familière, en présence d'un Dieu dont le regard épie
> jusqu'à nos songes ... Le jansénisme qui enlève tout à
> l'homme pour ne diminuer en rien la puissance de l'Etre
> infini, et qui accoutume un jeune être à vivre dans le
> tremblement, a laissé plus de traces qu'on n'imagine, au
> fond de nos provinces. (*4*, p.61)

Mauriac's mother believed fervently that sex was sinful, and her children were taught to be constantly on their guard against 'mauvaises pensées'. God demanded both purity and an exclusive love. Yet Mauriac now, in 1926, believed that his vocation as a novelist required him to explore those hitherto repressed areas of his personality. Several years of living in a Parisian society which was characterized by behaviour that he had been brought up to consider sinful — abuse of drink and drugs, adultery, homosexuality, greed in all its forms — had not been without effect, and the influence of people like Gide, Cocteau and Radiguet had been considerable. In 1926 Mauriac had just turned forty. His deepest beliefs and attachments were being called into question by his vocation, by his lifestyle, and conceivably by the possibility of new emotional relationships.

It certainly seems that during the first part of 1926 his emotions were in a tangle. The short story *Coups de couteau* was written that summer, at the same time as *Thérèse Desqueyroux*, and Mauriac later acknowledged that it was a fragment of a 'roman non écrit, que je ne pouvais pas écrire à ce moment-là, étant, si j'ose dire, trop contemporain du drame, trop directement brûlé par lui' (*1*, p.995). Its four brief chapters show us an artist called Louis (the name of Mauriac's uncle, used again in *Le Nœud de vipères*) hurting his wife by revealing his relationship with a young protégée of his. His wife then tries to make him jealous in return by evoking the memory of a near-romance with another of his admirers. Whether Mauriac the successful artist was tempted in the same way as Louis, or whether some recent experience revived memories of an earlier attachment, he was evidently made forcefully aware of the destructive power of sexual desire.

At the same time his links with the Jansenist version of Catholicism in which he had been brought up had been weakened by his immersion in Parisian society and, just as importantly, by his fervent devotion to his writing. *Thérèse Desqueyroux* was to be his fifth major novel in as many years. Writing can be a serious distraction from prayer and religious devotion, as the curé d'Ambricourt was to find in Bernanos's *Journal d'un curé de campagne*. In April 1928 Gide was to give a particularly probing formulation to the contradiction in which Mauriac found himself: 'En somme, ce que vous cherchez, c'est la permission d'être chrétien sans avoir à brûler vos livres ... Compromis rassurant qui permette d'aimer Dieu sans perdre de vue Mammon'.[5]

Thérèse Desqueyroux was the first novel to come out of this inner turmoil. Thérèse's exploration of her inner world can be seen plausibly in terms of Mauriac's own self-questioning. It would obviously be naïve to equate the two: Thérèse is a fictional creation, a youngish woman with a non-Christian background, while Mauriac is a real person, an older man with a strongly Catholic background. Nevertheless, through the intermediary of Thérèse, Mauriac is able

---

[5] Letter reproduced in *Correspondance Gide-Mauriac* (*Cahiers André Gide*, 2, Paris, Gallimard, 1971), pp.75-77.

to undertake a journey back through the darkness associated with fear of sexuality and perhaps with the anxiety of birth itself, to a place whose name, Saint-Clair, echoes that of his own mother, Claire, and to a house which may represent the womb: plunged in darkness and cut off from the outside world by water (see *23*). A psychoanalytical approach to the text reveals a tension which may be in part Mauriac's own, between the 'besoin de s'accrocher à la mère désespérément absente' and the desire to turn in on the self in silence and coldness: there is an 'oscillation du discours mauriacien entre l'excès de contact, fusionnel, et l'excès de distance, schizoïde, qui empêchent chacun d'être un lieu, avec les autres et dans le monde' (*39*, pp.140-41).

Some Antecedents

But Mauriac had other starting points for his novel besides his own immediate situation. In *Le Roman* he claimed to be writing consciously within a literary tradition. As well as exploiting the individualism of Dostoevsky, Gide and perhaps Barrès, Mauriac probably had both Zola and Racine in mind. He also demonstrated a strong sense of continuity with his previous novel, *Le Désert de l'amour* (1925).

The very title of Mauriac's novel *Thérèse Desqueyroux* suggests that it may be a response to Zola's *Thérèse Raquin* of 1867.[6] Both are penetrating psychological studies of a woman haunted by her past. Murder and indeed poison feature in both, as does the figure of the old, infirm woman who silently watches what is going on. But whereas Zola was concerned to illustrate a particular theory, Mauriac is dealing with a person. Zola's declared intention was: 'étant donné un homme puissant et une femme inassouvie, chercher en eux la bête, ne voir même que la bête, les jeter dans un drame violent, et noter scrupuleusement les sensations et les actes de ces êtres'.[7] The end of *Thérèse Raquin* shows Thérèse and Laurent

---

[6] Gaston Duthuron (*6*, pp.174-77) compares *Thérèse Raquin* and *Le Baiser au lépreux*.

[7] Emile Zola, *Thérèse Raquin* (Paris, Le Livre de poche, 1970), pp.8-9.

crying, 'sans parler, songeant à la vie de boue qu'ils avaient menée et qu'ils mèneraient encore, s'ils étaient assez lâches pour vivre',[8] before both drinking poison. Mauriac's Foreword seems to be in part a response to Zola. The epigraph, taken from Baudelaire, calls into question the rigid categories with which Zola operates: 'O Créateur! peut-il exister des monstres aux yeux de Celui-là seul qui sait pourquoi i¹s existent, comment ils *se sont faits*, et comment ils auraient pu *ne pas se faire* ...' (p.5/5). Mauriac then takes up Zola's image of the 'vie de boue', and expresses his sympathetic under-standing in contrast to his predecessor's cold 'travail analytique': 'Beaucoup s'étonneront que j'aie pu imaginer une créature plus odieuse encore que tous mes autres héros ... Les "cœurs sur la main" n'ont pas d'histoire; mais je connais celle des cœurs enfouis et tout mêlés à un corps de boue' (p.7/6). Part of Mauriac's aim, then, may have been to rewrite *Thérèse Raquin* from a more sympathetic, human perspective, and also within a provincial context (which links his Thérèse with Emma Bovary). A much more powerful and positive influence on *Thérèse Desqueyroux* was Racine, and in particular his *Phèdre* of 1677.

In the Preface which Mauriac wrote in 1951 for volume VIII of his complete works, the volume which includes his *Vie de Jean Racine*, there is this sentence:

> Ainsi, dès le collège, suis-je entré plus qu'aucun de mes camarades dans le miracle de Racine, ai-je été pénétré jusqu'aux moelles, oserais-je dire, par son pathétique, de sorte que mes romans — pour leur malheur et pour leur condamnation, penseront certains de mes critiques — procèdent évidemment de ses tragédies. (*4*, p.ii)

As it stands, that is a general remark, referring to all Mauriac's novels, and to a tone rather than to any details of plot or character. That in itself is worth noting. *Thérèse Desqueyroux* is a novel in which tone — style and atmosphere — is of primary importance. The tragic sense of destiny is Racinian: the narrowness of focus, the

---

[8] ibid., p.245.

unity of time in the first ten chapters, the oppressive environment, the powerful elemental imagery, are all reminiscent of Racine's theatre. Sartre, one of Mauriac's harshest critics, drew attention to the Racinian flavour of *La Fin de la nuit* in order to condemn it as a novel: the 'goût de la concision', the theatrical dialogue ('Ne songez-vous pas aux fureurs d'Hermione?'), even the structure (see *42*, pp.53-54).[9]

Mauriac then went on, in the Preface to the next volume, to indicate the particular fascination that *Phèdre* held for him, to the extent that its influence 'apparaît dans le filigrane de presque tous mes récits' (*3*, p.929). Certainly he had used some elements of it as the starting point for *Le Désert de l'amour*. In his notes on the first draft of that novel, Jacques Petit observes that:

> C'est le personnage de la femme qui devait être au centre du roman ... Ce personnage de femme, amoureuse d'un jeune homme passionné de sports, dédaigneux de toute conquête, c'est Phèdre devant Hippolyte — il ne manque pas même le lien familial qui donne à cette passion un caractère incestueux, sans toutefois la rendre impossible. Un 'drame terrible' devait se produire ... On imagine volontiers que la mort du jeune homme eût été, comme dans *Phèdre*, et dans *Destins*, le dénouement. (*1*, p.1319)

Between *Le Désert de l'amour* and *Destins* came *Thérèse Desqueyroux* and *La Vie de Jean Racine*. The latter work gives an important place to *Phèdre*. The features of the play to which Mauriac draws attention are: the concentration on the figure of Phèdre herself; the 'penchant d'une femme déjà au déclin pour un jeune être intact'; her fear of incest; her awareness of being 'un moment de sa race' as well as a responsible individual; her 'prodigieuse lucidité'; and the absence of divine love and grace in her universe ('aucune goutte de

---

[9]C.D.E. Tolton (*52*) notes the prevalence in Mauriac's novels of the *revirement*, the Racinian structural device of the interjection of false hopes before the final fall. In *Thérèse Desqueyroux* the *revirement* is used to give tragic intensity.

sang n'a été versée pour cette âme') (*4*, pp.103-06). All except the second and third of these (which are present in *Destins*) find their echo in *Thérèse Desqueyroux*, although it could be argued that it is Thérèse's search for self-knowledge that is prodigious, rather than her actual lucidity. Mauriac does not mention Thérèse explicitly in *La Vie de Jean Racine*, but there are two passages where he seems to have her in mind:

> Phèdre traîne après elle une immense postérité d'êtres qui savent ne pouvoir rien attendre ni espérer, exilés de tout amour, sur une terre déserte, sous un ciel d'airain. Nous retrouvons, à chaque tournant de notre route, sa figure morte, ses lèvres sèches, ses yeux brûlés qui demandent grâce; tristes corps perclus de honte et dont le seul crime est d'être au monde. (*4*, p.106)[10]

> Les créatures sur qui pèsent de lourdes fatalités sont, en effet, les mêmes qui souhaitent le plus ardemment de mourir et de renaître. Nul ne les délivrera de leur corps de boue, hors Celui qui pour cela d'abord est venu en ce monde. (*4*, p.144)

These two passages speak of lostness, lovelessness and grace denied: 'Thérèse Desqueyroux, comme Phèdre, se confond avec le visage de la désespérance' (*35*, p.118). Julie Bellade, Thérèse's disgraced grandmother, is also a Phèdre-figure, whose function, at least in part, is to reveal Thérèse's destiny to her. Thérèse, then, like Phèdre, 'a le malheur de pleinement connaître le destin funeste qui l'asservit, comme le personnage racinien, elle est porteuse de mort' (*35*, p.117).

Phèdre is not named in *Thérèse Desqueyroux*, but there are two allusions to the play. One is a strong verbal reminiscence: Thérèse's 'Que lui dirait-elle? par quel aveu commencer?' (p.19/22) can hardly help recalling Phèdre's 'Ciel! que lui vais-je dire? Et par

---

[10] Compare the epigraph from Thomas Mann which Mauriac had originally planned to use for *Thérèse Desqueyroux*: '... certains êtres s'égarent nécessairement parce qu'il n'y a pas pour eux de vrais chemins' (see *2*, p.929).

où commencer?' (I.iii.247). The other is a reference to Hippolyte. Early on in the novel Thérèse smiles at her caricatural memories of Bernard as a young man, and remembers that 'adolescent, il n'était point si laid, cet Hippolyte mal léché — moins curieux des jeunes filles que du lièvre qu'il forçait dans la lande' (p.27/33). The Hippolytus of Euripides had been 'un adolescent chaste, trop chaste, un enfant qui court les forêts ... ennemi de toutes les femmes' (*4*, p.103), even if Racine was to give him a secret love. The purpose of this reference, then, is twofold: to emphasize Bernard's affinity with the natural world (and corresponding lack of interest in humans, especially women), and to make us think of the contrasting complexity of Thérèse-Phèdre.

Thérèse is therefore more than a social rebel or an expression of Mauriac's inner tensions. For Jacques Monférier,

> certes révélatrice des mesquineries de son milieu social, Thérèse Desqueyroux n'en est pas moins un être réprouvé, marqué de toute éternité, expression mythique du désespoir plus que de la révolte, voué à la destruction et à la mort, annonciateur du néant plus que de l'espérance. (*35*, p.118)

It is not only the link between the characters of Phèdre and Thérèse that confirms the Racinian flavour of *Thérèse Desqueyroux*, however. Mauriac evidently identified himself strongly with the Racine of the period 1675-77:

> Nous ne savons presque rien de ce que fut sa vie cachée de 1675 à 1677; mais cette *Phèdre* conçue durant ces années mystérieuses, de quelle expérience nous apparaît-elle chargée! ... Racine communique à Phèdre, durant les années qu'elle se forme en lui, cette certitude fatale au bonheur humain, que l'amour charnel est le mal, le mal que nous ne pouvons pas ne pas commettre. (*4*, pp.99-100)

There are two points here. One is that Mauriac saw the writing of *Phèdre* as associated with a period of crisis in Racine's life, just as the writing of *Thérèse Desqueyroux* was with a crisis in his own. Both authors shared that 'instinct créateur' which 'nous pousse à mettre en lumière, à fixer le plus obscur, le plus trouble de nous-mêmes' (*4*, p.108). But Racine then stopped writing, fearing that his inner turmoil might harm his work. He had the excuse of artistic perfection and the hierarchy of genres: 'La tragédie racinienne est d'abord netteté et clarté. Elle ne saurait prétendre à exprimer ce qui, dans l'homme, relève des genres humains les moins purs' (*4*, p.108). Mauriac has no such excuse, and cannot repudiate his painful vocation of self-examination. The critics who hailed *Thérèse Desqueyroux* as Mauriac's *Phèdre*, meaning by that the pinnacle of his literary career, did not realize what an ironically apt comment they were making. Mauriac conveys something of his anguish in *La Vie de Jean Racine*:

> Un roi de France dirait aujourd'hui à tel ou tel: 'Laissez là votre roman annuel, je vous nomme gentilhomme de ma chambre et vous ne ferez plus rien que de raconter mes exploits...' Ah! qu'il quitterait de bon cœur son écritoire! Surtout si sa jeunesse ne fut pas toute pure, si d'inquiétantes figures rôdent autour de lui, s'il a le sentiment que le sol est miné sous ses pas. (*4*, p.109)

The second point is that *Thérèse Desqueyroux*, like Phèdre, is a development of previous characters. After completing *Iphigénie*, says Mauriac,

> Racine résistera deux années encore à la femme qu'à plusieurs reprises il a mise au monde, et qui demande une fois encore à renaître ... Le certain est que sa créature, qu'il porte plus longtemps que les autres, se nourrit aussi de lui-même plus que n'ont fait Hermione et Roxane. (*4*, p.99)

Thérèse, like Phèdre, is a person carried and nourished by her creator as a mother carries her baby and nourishes it with her own substance. The gestation has been a long one. In an early draft of Mauriac's previous novel, *Le Désert de l'amour*, the main character was already to be called Thérèse (later changed to Maria Cross). Thérèse/Maria comes from Saint-Clair, like Thérèse Desqueyroux. Mauriac later recognized that both the family environment and the character herself foreshadowed *Thérèse Desqueyroux*:

> L'espèce de rancœur que la vie de famille avait
> accumulée en moi ... cette rancœur qui devait se délivrer
> dans *Thérèse Desqueyroux* et dans *Le Nœud de vipères*,
> s'exprime ici déjà ... Quant au personnage de Maria
> Cross, la femme entretenue, il m'apparaît comme une
> ébauche de la créature que je portais en moi et qui allait
> devenir Thérèse Desqueyroux. (*1*, p.993)

Maria discovers her own solitude and initiates Raymond Courrèges and his father into theirs, in the 'desert de l'amour'. She realizes that she is not 'à la mesure du plaisir'. Thérèse, too, will be incapable of forming satisfying relationships, and her effect on other people will be even more destructive.

The figure of Thérèse, then, while she embodies something of the 'confusion' and 'remous' (*4*, p.108) of Mauriac's own personal experience, can also be placed in the context of a literary tradition. The Foreword to *Thérèse Desqueyroux* suggests that Mauriac also drew on models that he had himself observed in the world of provincial society. In particular, he recalls having seen in his youth, 'dans une salle étouffante d'assises, livrée aux avocats moins féroces que les dames empanachées, ta petite figure blanche et sans lèvres' (p.5). He later confirmed that 'Thérèse est née de la vision que j'ai gardée d'une dame empoisonneuse entrevue sur le banc des Assises à Bordeaux' (*1*, p.993). The Canaby Affair had been the talk of Bordeaux in May 1906, when Mauriac was 20. Henriette-Blanche Canaby, wife of a respectable wine-broker, and very much part of the polite society of Bordeaux (she even had some literary pretensions), spent four days in the dock accused of administering poison to her husband who had nearly died as a result. Towards the end of April 1905 she had acquired considerable quantities of aconitine, digitalin and chloroform by means of forged prescriptions, and a few days later her husband, already ill, had suddenly taken a turn for the worse after drinking his morning chocolate. She had at first refused to let anyone see him, but when, at the point of death, he was removed from the family home and taken to a *maison de santé*, his health had improved dramatically. During the course of the investigation it emerged that Mme Canaby had also obtained three bottles of Fowler's solution, a remedy with a high arsenic content. Yet the family seemed to be happy as well as respectable, despite a suspiciously close friendship between Mme Canaby and a wealthy bachelor who used to take her and her daughters on holiday. At the trial M. Canaby testified in favour of his wife, even going so far as to deny a number of details about his illness that seemed to be established facts. After a moving speech by Maître Peyrecave, in which he turned the charge of criminality back on the prosecution, claiming that what was at stake was the honour of the family, Mme Canaby was acquitted of attempted murder, though she was given a prison sentence for forgery (see 6, pp.22-26; 28, pp.208-10).

Many of the details of the case, including the specific poisons and even the name of the defending counsel, have been faithfully transcribed in Mauriac's novel. Yet he is not interested in the case as such, which is dismissed on the very first page. What is important for Mauriac is the deadlock in which the protagonists find themselves even after that dismissal, and above all the mind of Thérèse herself, who is not only 'the poisoner whose act of quiet passion momentarily disturbs, even if it can never shatter, the implacable calm of a smug community' (6, p.26), but a much more complex and fascinating 'monstre'.

4. The World of Thérèse

We are now in a better position to appreciate that complexity. It would be a mistake, however, to think that a literary text can be fully explained by outside influences and possible models, or by the author's stated intentions or biographical experiences. The world of Thérèse is the world of the text, although that will of course have been conditioned by the factors discussed in the previous chapter. It is to the text that we must now return.

One of the most obvious features of the text is the shifting point of view. In the Foreword there is an authorial voice addressing Thérèse. The first chapter then starts in traditional third-person mode with an omniscient narrator describing Thérèse leaving the court-house. This narrator has access to her thoughts and feelings: we are told that she can feel the mist on her face, and that she is afraid someone may be waiting for her. There is some dialogue in direct speech, but there is also indirect discourse. 'Oui, la petite place semblait déserte' is presumably what Thérèse is thinking. Her father's reply to her question about the carriage is recorded in indirect form: 'son père l'avait fait attendre sur la route de Budos, en dehors de la ville, pour ne pas attirer l'attention'. It is not always clear who is responsible for this indirect discourse. Is it Thérèse or her father who says, or thinks: 'Heureusement, les jours avaient bien diminué'? Are we to hear the narrator's voice in a comment like: 'Elle aspira de nouveau la nuit pluvieuse, comme un être menacé d'étouffement'? And what about the use of the future tense and of the image of water later in the same paragraph? 'Marie, à cette heure, déjà s'endort dans une chambre d'Argelouse où Thérèse arrivera tard, ce soir; alors la jeune femme ... se penchera, et ses lèvres chercheront comme de l'eau, cette vie endormie' (p.12/11). The point of view appears to shift in the course of the sentence, from Thérèse to an omniscient narrator who imposes his vision by means of the image. The point of view continues to be unstable throughout the novel. Some sections are written in the third person while largely espousing Thérèse's point of view; others are so dominated by her point of view that they are printed in inverted commas, using the first person (e.g. much of Chapters VI, VII and VIII). We are also given the thoughts of other characters, for instance those of Bernard in Chapter XII before Thérèse enters the room. Very occasionally Thérèse herself is addressed in the second person, although it is not clear (except in the Foreword) who is speaking, and whether the voice that is addressing her is in some measure her own.

Writing mainly about the sequel to *Thérèse Desqueyroux*, *La Fin de la nuit*, Sartre complained that Mauriac was violating an essential law of novelistic creation in the ambiguous attitude he adopted towards his characters: 'le romancier peut être leur témoin ou leur complice, jamais les deux à la fois' (*42*, p.48). But that was precisely what Mauriac was trying to be. At times the narrative point of view was so close to Thérèse that the 'elle' was virtually a 'je', but then it would move right away and define her as an object with no freedom, saddled with qualities and a destiny that the novelist had imposed on her. Sartre later recognized that he had failed to appreciate that all literary techniques are 'des truquages'.[11] The author-narrator can never be entirely absent from the text, even when the point of view appears to be exclusively that of the character. For Jacques Petit, 'l'étonnement de Sartre nous étonne, aujourd'hui que la critique et les romanciers nous ont appris à nous méfier des leurres romanesques: il n'y a pas de personnages (indépendants, libres, coupés de leur créateur) et nous n'entendons jamais qu'une voix, celle de l'auteur' (*1*, pp.lxxxvi-lxxxvii).

André Joubert finds a justification for the intervention of voices other than that of Thérèse's own subjectivity in the fact that 'cette subjectivité en vient à renoncer en partie à elle-même' (*26*, p.186). She refuses to face up to her past actions or to her present responsibilities, and the result is 'une dépossession progressive du

---

[11] See Michel Contat and Michel Rybalka, *Les Ecrits de Sartre* (Paris, Gallimard, 1970), p.73.

personnage de ses privilèges d'intériorité, à proportion du développement de sa mauvaise foi'. The novel is about failure, and so it is entirely appropriate that at the level of narrative technique the point of view of Thérèse should be gradually overwhelmed by that of the third-person narrator. Indeed Joubert interprets Mauriac's use of both third-person and second-person forms as a way of emphasizing 'les contraintes qui pèsent sur la condition de Thérèse'. The narrative voice which addresses her, for instance at the end of Chapter VII, is comparable to those other voices, attributed to identifiable characters, which are constantly urging her to take stock of her situation and do something about it: 'Tu vas trop loin, Thérèse' (Bernard, p.42/57); 'Trouve autre chose, Thérèse' (her father, p.84/118). She has brought all these voices upon herself. At the same time we, as readers, need to see what is happening to Thérèse as she collapses into 'mauvaise foi' and passivity: hence the comments on her appearance and behaviour from the narrator and from other characters such as the housekeeper Balionte.

Joubert's analysis has the merit of doing justice to the formal quality of the literary text, but the judgment he makes on Thérèse as a failure seems too clear-cut. André Séailles adopts a more supple approach:

> Les procédés narratifs attestent une participation au destin de Thérèse plus qu'une domination ... Le jeu des points de vue avec leur subtilité et leur complexité quasi musicale fonctionne comme une poétique plutôt que comme une logique. (*46*, pp.58-59)

For him it is not the contrast between different points of view but rather their continuing interplay that is important. Paul Croc goes further, claiming that 'le point de vue peut être considéré comme le sujet même' of the novel (*16*, p.34). James Reid even sees the shifting point of view as 'calling into question the very notion that the text represents or constitutes actions or events: its narrativity' (*41*, p.167). Arthur Holmberg remains on the level of character when he observes that 'pour Thérèse les frontières entre le moi et l'autre ont tendance à s'estomper' (*25*, p.129). It certainly seems as though no clear opposition can be maintained between interiority and exteriority, between subjectivity and objectivity. That does not, however, totally solve the problem of the relationship between author and character, which is felt most acutely in the Foreword, and which will be discussed later.

Another notable feature of the text is the 'flashback' technique. The account of Thérèse's journey in the first eight chapters acts as a framework for a series of 'retours en arrière' or 'plongées' (Mauriac's own term: see *2*, p.1048). This is effective as a device for holding the reader's attention, after the opening *in medias res*. We are eager to find out how Thérèse has come to the point of poisoning her husband. The novelist Roger Martin du Gard, who won the Nobel Prize for Literature in 1937, found it all too artificial and slow:

> Pourquoi ... vous donner tant de mal, combiner tous ces moyens de locomotion archi-lents, afin de nous faire avaler toute l'histoire, toute la vie de Thérèse, en ayant l'air de nous raconter simplement le parcours qu'elle fait? Comme vous attachez de l'importance à truquer vos 'présentations'! Croyez-vous qu'il y a moins d'art à aborder de face ces questions-là? (D'ailleurs vous avouez presque que c'est uniquement pour le lecteur que vous faites ainsi reconstruire à votre Thérèse son passé, puisque, au moment de se servir de ses souvenirs repêchés, votre héroïne y renonce.) (*30*, p.360)

It has been suggested that Mauriac was deliberately making use of a technique borrowed from the cinema, although it also has a perfectly good literary pedigree. Interestingly, Georges Franju in his 1962 film of *Thérèse Desqueyroux* made a point of not using flashbacks as such: the barriers between past and present are completely broken down, and everything becomes present (see *34*, p.155). It is striking, too, that the fragments of Thérèse's past that come back to her are arranged in a strictly chronological order, beginning with her childhood and going up to a few months before the narrative present. That is not only a convenient solution for the novelist (though it is certainly that), but it is in keeping with Thérèse's desire to produce a coherent, ordered account of her life for herself and for Bernard, and it is also in keeping with a sense of destiny. A series of random flashbacks might have been more 'realistic', more like the stream of consciousness being exploited by some of Mauriac's contemporaries, but it would have been less appropriate to the character of Thérèse, who is methodical enough to insist on reading Anne's letters 'dans l'ordre' (p.37/49), and to the atmosphere of inevitability that Mauriac is trying to create. In fact the potential rigidity of the chronological scheme is softened by its fragmentation, by the shifting point of view, and by the appearance of other images from the past which are only loosely tied to that scheme. Thus the vision of the 'visage inconnu' of Thérèse's grandmother Julie Bellade and the evocation of Anne in Chapter II both occur before Thérèse has begun to 'tout reprendre depuis le commencement' (p.21/25). Later we come across the echo of comments that continued to be made in the neighbourhood long after the day of the wedding (p.34/44), and another childhood memory of Anne in the middle of Thérèse's recollection of her honeymoon (p.41/56).

It is easy to focus on the interplay of past and present, and forget the future. Thérèse's whole process of recollection is undertaken under the pressure of the forthcoming meeting with Bernard, and that immediate future colours the first eight chapters of the novel. Bernard will fulfil the function of a magistrate much more effectively than the one who has just dismissed the case, and it is to him that she must answer. The nightmarish quality of her situation is emphasized by the episode at the beginning of Chapter II when she actually falls asleep and dreams that the magistrate has found the packet of poison. From Chapter IX, when the meeting with Bernard fails to produce the expected climax, the future recedes and becomes indeterminate, but it still provides an important pole of Thérèse's meditation: 'Le premier jour de mauvais temps... Combien devrait-elle en vivre au coin de cette cheminée où le feu mourait? ... Tout ce jour à vivre encore dans cette chambre; et puis ces semaines, ces mois...' (p.103/146). She constructs possible scenarios for the future, installing herself in them (when the imperfect tense is used: e.g. 'Elle enchantait un cercle de visages attentifs', p.105/149), and then standing back to contemplate them from a distance, when the future tense and the conditional and infinitive moods take over:

> ...comment imaginer qu'il puisse un jour ne plus pleuvoir? Il pleuvra jusqu'à la fin du monde. Si elle avait de l'argent, elle se sauverait à Paris, irait droit chez Jean Azévédo, se confierait à lui; il saurait lui procurer du travail. Etre une femme seule dans Paris, qui gagne sa vie, qui ne dépend de personne... Etre sans famille! (p.106/150)

In Chapter XII the future again becomes more definite, with the promise of liberation once Anne is safely married. In the final chapter, with that promise realized, Thérèse is still turned towards the future, making plans, discarding certain possibilities in favour of others. At the same time, of course, she is looking backwards, evoking specific details of her life with Bernard and of the landscape that she has left behind. The term 'plongées', then, is better than 'flashbacks' or 'retours en arrière', since Thérèse's meditation is characterized by anticipations of the future as well as by evocations of the past.

It is also characterized by a certain atemporality. If the journey from B. to Argelouse takes roughly as long to read about as it does to undertake in reality, there is no consistency about the representation of real time in the novel. The period of Thérèse's engagement is covered briefly, whereas the last evening of the honeymoon is described at length. The first few days back at Saint-Clair are again evoked in detail, with the rest of the summer being dismissed in a couple of pages. Part of the explanation is that Mauriac, like a dramatist, concentrates on the most significant episodes. Yet some major events are mentioned only in passing or not at all: the wedding, the birth of Marie, the first time that Thérèse deliberately put Bernard's medicine in his glass before he arrived to ensure that he would take a double dose... Real, chronological time is replaced not necessarily by psychological time (since the world of Thérèse is larger than her consciousness or even her subconscious), but by an atemporal mood or atmosphere which is evoked with more or less intensity. It is true that the first summer of Thérèse's marriage is dismissed in a couple of pages, but the reader none the less gains a strong impression of the invasion of life by death, and that is what matters. Thérèse feels 'torpeur' and 'hébétude', longs for 'repos' and 'sommeil', and comments that 'la vie des gens de notre espèce ressemble déjà terriblement à la mort' (p.57/77). Bernard himself is obsessed by a 'peur de la mort', and is compared to a rotten tree or a cracked girder (p.56/75). The temporal concentration intensifies the mood.

While it is perfectly possible to reconstruct the temporal sequence of events (although not their exact timing), that broad sweep fails to establish any convincing causal links. All that Thérèse can do for Bernard is 'lui rappeler point par point comment la chose arriva' (p.80/111). Yet she has already recognized that 'quand j'aurai atteint avec lui ce défilé où me voilà, tout me restera encore à découvrir' (p.47/63), so that it is hardly surprising when 'toute son histoire, péniblement reconstruite, s'effondre' (p.86/119). What is left is a mood, the double sense of anxiety and destiny that has been there from the start.

As Bernard Swift has pointed out, the 'mere structural device of introducing the crime as *having already happened*' (*50*, p.43) creates a sense of the inevitable, of Thérèse's destiny as a bearer of death (cf. *35*, p.117). Bernard Chochon sees her as trying to resist that destiny by resisting the very passage of time, attempting to 'figer les aiguilles de son temps intérieur sur un éternel présent' (7, p.192). For Chochon, the long passages of meditation and reflection have a serenity about them which contrasts sharply with the brisk, harsh evocations of 'le temps de la grisaille quotidienne, vécu dans l'incommunicabilité conjugale' (7, p.189). This oscillation between *adagio* and *allegro* is the expression of a 'moi obsessionnel' trying to come to terms with time. It is no accident if what sticks in our mind is the image of Thérèse with a cigarette, 'cette éternelle cigarette négligemment suspendue aux lèvres de l'héroïne, en signe d'indifférence à l'égard de son entourage, manière bien à elle, déjà, de rendre le temps supportable et, à défaut de pouvoir le *tuer*, du moins de l'alléger en essayant de cohabiter avec lui' (*6*, p.183).

If, then, there are no clear frontiers between the different points of view or between past, present and future, and if what the text presents us with is a 'moi obsessionnel' which is larger than a single consciousness, we can start exploring the world of Thérèse without being limited by the traditional idea of character. Indeed, if we attempt a character-sketch we find that the figure of Thérèse dissolves into the text: as I said at the beginning of this chapter, the world of Thérèse is the world of the text.

We are given some details about Thérèse's external appearance. We do not know her age, although Bernard is twenty-six when they get married (pp.26, 44 / 32, 60).[12] She is taller than her father (p.10/8), with a small head (pp.16, 32 / 19, 41), a short nose (p.127/183), prominent cheekbones (pp.17, 127 / 19, 183), rather large ears (p.98/138), and most strikingly, a 'large front, magnifique' (p.17/19). She has a pale complexion (p.78/108) but a 'beau sourire'

---

[12] In the film, Thérèse is portrayed by Emmanuelle Riva as a mature woman. The indications given in *La Fin de la nuit* are inconsistent with *Thérèse Desqueyroux*: Jacques Petit notes that ' Thérèse, qui s'est mariée jeune, à peine sortie du lycée, se trouve, dix-huit ans plus tard, âgée de quarante-cinq ans' (*3*, p.1001, n.6). Perhaps influenced by the film and by *La Fin de la nuit*, critics (e.g. Flower in *23*) have tended to see the Thérèse of *Thérèse Desqueyroux* as a little older than Bernard, twenty-seven or twenty-eight, without taking into account the implication of the first part of Petit's comment. Séailles (*46*, p.60) points out that Thérèse may be eighteen or twenty-eight at the time of her marriage: the text is not clear. But if Thérèse is in fact 'à peine sortie du lycée', and is thus several years younger than Bernard, that might help to explain his patronizing attitude, as well as some of her own adolescent characteristics. She is after all presented as being only slightly older than Anne. Before his marriage, Bernard treats Anne as too young to bother about (p.25/31). Thérèse also thinks of Anne as 'petite', and even represents her to Bernard on their honeymoon as 'une petite fille' (p.40/54). On the other hand, as suggested above (see p.16), Thérèse and Anne can be seen as two facets of the same character, which would imply a similarity in age. Anne was at the convent-school when Thérèse was at the *lycée*. When Bernard is twenty-six, then, Anne might be eighteen and Thérèse twenty. (I am grateful to Bernard Swift for some of these ideas.)

(p.124/178), and she can give her voice 'certaines inflexions basses et rauques' (p.124/179) which Bernard used to like. More than any of these physical features, however, what people notice about her is that 'on ne se demande pas si elle est jolie ou laide, on subit son charme' (p.19/23). It is true that on her wedding day she seemed 'laide et même affreuse', and that is said to have been in some way a revelation of her 'vrai visage' (pp.34/44-45), but she is more often presented as attractive and even having a certain dignity or grandeur (p.17/19). We do not know what clothes she likes wearing, apart from sandals in the country (p.65/90) and a tight-fitting suit in Paris (p.127/183). She smokes 'comme un sapeur' (p.30/38), and her smoking seems so much a part of her that it is a surprise to discover that almost all the references to it were added by Mauriac at a late stage (see 2, p.985: n.2 to p.88). It is certainly well integrated into the text, being linked with nonconformity, revolt, fire, destruction and sexuality.

More important than physical attributes — which in some cases are viewed subjectively and may be misleading — are Thérèse's attitudes of mind. Unlike Anne and the other members of her society, she likes reading, although she is unfamiliar with the authors mentioned by Jean Azévédo. She is sufficiently independent-minded to acknowledge her own complexity, recognizing within herself the seeds of the most socially and morally reprehensible actions, but without necessarily taking responsibility for them. She is thus a monster in terms of social expectations. Yet she craves purity, admires what is 'supérieur', and likes to feel that she belongs to an élite. In many ways she exhibits the characteristics of an adolescent. She preserves her solitude fiercely, putting on a mask to hide her feelings or else expressing them in the form of *boutades* which others ignore or at any rate fail to comprehend (p.78/107), but she also feels attracted to other solitary figures like the village priest. In her meditation on existence the word *néant* and its compounds *anéantir* and *anéantissement* occur several times. There is the *néant* of her present situation, seen as either neutral, allowing her to create something to fill it, or negative: 'Inutilité de ma vie — néant de ma vie — solitude sans bornes — destinée sans issue' (p.87/120, cf.

pp.57, 79/77, 109). There is the *néant* of death, which appears alternately welcoming and frightening ('elle qui n'hésitait pas à y
précipiter autrui, se cabre devant le néant', p.99/139); and there is
anéantissement by the family, through voluntary self-sacrifice or
through expulsion. Thérèse offers to disappear like her grandmother
'comme si je n'avais jamais été' (p.89/124), and although Bernard
refuses to listen to her, that is effectively what happens. As he says:
'vous n'êtes plus rien; ce qui existe, c'est le nom que vous portez,
hélas!' (p.92/128).

That brings us back to the title of the novel. 'Thérèse
Desqueyroux' proves to be simply a label. The text proposes
different (but incomplete, and sometimes mutually exclusive) ways
of creating the person who bears that name. The decks are cleared in
the opening paragraph of Chapter I, when the lawyer opens a door
and announces: 'Non-lieu ... il n'y a personne'. If we were tempted,
because of the mention of the court-house, or because of the Foreword, or because of some prior knowledge of the work, to label
Thérèse as a criminal, that option is removed straight away. The case
has been dropped. But more than that, the text seems to be creating a
tabula rasa. Everything that follows will be provisional: not only the
story which Thérèse prepares and which 's'effondre' at the beginning
of Chapter IX, but the whole attempt to construct a logical character
around the few known facts.

Several environments are proposed for Thérèse. She is first
presented as having a natural affinity with the mist. In the second
sentence we are told that she 'sentit sur sa face la brume et,
profondément, l'aspira' (p.9/7). This image is taken up and
developed, so that Thérèse not only continues to breathe in the damp
air ('elle aspira de nouveau la nuit pluvieuse', pp.11-12/11; 'sa
poitrine dilatée s'emplit de brouillard', p.18/21), but she acquires an
aura of mist:

> Elle apercevait les êtres et les choses et son
> propre corps et son esprit même, ainsi qu'un mirage,
> une vapeur suspendue en dehors d'elle. (p.79/109)

> Il fallait ... que la chambre baignât dans une
> brume qu'avait aspirée et rejetée sa bouche. (p.109/155)

When she muses that 'elle a été aspirée par le crime' (p.82/114), it is as if she herself is the mist and her crime the substantial reality at the centre. One could apply to her Baudelaire's observation: 'De la vaporisation et de la centralisation du *moi*: tout est là'.[13] That is indeed the problem: there is *vaporisation*, but there is also *centralisation*, and her *moi* cannot conveniently be absorbed into some other entity such as the family: 'Mais moi, mais moi, mais moi...' (p.97/136, cf. p.115/165). A more natural destiny for her would be absorption by something more akin to the mist: a pool, a river, or the sea. All three figure in the novel as possible goals. Thérèse fails to escape to the ocean, although the sound of the wind in the trees makes it seem very present; she admits that she would never have the courage to drown herself 'dans l'eau d'une lagune' like the shepherd (see p.125/180); but it is striking that in a sense she does finally reach a river. Paris is consistently presented in the final chapter in terms of a river, with 'le flot humain', 'd'invisibles écluses', 'la vague des taxis', and the culminating image of 'le fleuve humain, cette masse vivante qui allait s'ouvrir sous son corps, la rouler, l'entraîner' (pp.120-25/172-80).

After the mist, a second environment is that of the night. Night arrives in the first chapter even before Thérèse reaches the *calèche* which will take her to the station, and does not end until the close of Chapter X. Even then her imprisonment is dominated by evocations of the night. The final chapter, which is set on 'un matin chaud de mars', ends with Thérèse seeing the 'forêt vivante' of Paris in terms of 'le gémissement des pins d'Argelouse, la nuit' (p.128/184). Night is obviously associated with obscurity, imprisonment, violence, anxiety and insecurity, but it also has positive connotations. It is a time when the sounds of the natural world come into their own: windows are opened, and the wind brings a 'bruit d'Océan' (pp.102, 109/145, 155). There is a certain complicity between Thérèse and the

---

[13] Charles Baudelaire, 'Mon cœur mis à nu', in *Œuvres complètes*, I (Paris, Gallimard: Bibliothèque de la Pléiade , 1975), p.676.

night. Indeed, she says to Bernard: 'La forêt ne me fait pas peur, ni les ténèbres. Elles me connaissent; nous nous connaissons' (p.89/124).

The ambivalence of these two environments, the mist and the night, is shown by a striking passage which comes just as Thérèse's train approaches Saint-Clair at the end of its journey through the night. She is recalling the previous autumn, when Bernard was so ill: 'Elle traversait, seule, un tunnel, vertigineusement; elle en était au plus obscur; il fallait, sans réfléchir, comme une brute, sortir de ces ténèbres, de cette fumée, atteindre l'air libre, vite! vite!' (pp.83/115-16; see also *23*). This alternation between acceptance of her environment on the one hand, and anxiety and a sense of *étouffement* on the other, is fundamental to the world of Thérèse.

The desert is a further ambivalent environment. To begin with, the emphasis seems to be on a desert of love (*Le Désert de l'amour* was the title of Mauriac's previous novel). As she leaves the court-house, Thérèse notices that 'la petite place semblait déserte', despite the fact that the lawyer is accompanying her and that she has just recognized her father. Human company, even that of Anne, is at best fleeting: 'une créature s'évade hors de l'île déserte où tu imaginais qu'elle vivrait près de toi jusqu'à la fin; elle franchit l'abîme qui te sépare des autres, les rejoint' (p.41/56). On the other hand, a desert island has its attractions, at least potentially: Thérèse, at the end of her honeymoon, 'souhaitait de rentrer à Saint-Clair comme une déportée qui s'ennuie dans un cachot provisoire est curieuse de connaître l'île où doit se consumer ce qui lui reste de vie' (p.36/48). She comes to identify herself with her desert environment, as she does with the night: 'J'ai été créée à l'image de ce pays aride et où rien n'est vivant, hors les oiseaux qui passent, les sangliers nomades' (p.89/124).

The birds and the wild boar of that last quotation are hunted by men. Thérèse, as a creature of the mist, the night and the desert, is naturally at odds with human society, and is seen in terms of a frightened, hunted animal: 'elle avait peur d'être attendue, hésitait à sortir' (p.9/7); 'elle avait vécu, jusqu'à ce soir, d'être traquée' (p.16/19); 'bête tapie qui entend se rapprocher la meute' (p.84/117).

Bernard treats her as he treats any other *gibier*: the pigeons which he
brings home in a bag (p.70/95: an image powerfully exploited by
Georges Franju in his film of *Thérèse Desqueyroux*), or the wild sow
which he tries, unsuccessfully, to tame (p.118/169). Thérèse is not
merely hunted, but encircled, trapped, imprisoned (see *14*) — by the
family, by society, and even by the external world of the trees and
the rain in which she has sometimes felt at home: 'Comme si ce n'eût
pas été assez des pins innombrables, la pluie ininterrompue
multipliait autour de la sombre maison ses millions de barreaux
mouvants' (p.75/104). It is a constant theme of this novel that what is
at one moment a 'refuge' can become a 'cage' or a 'prison' the next.

    In the same way, the prey can also become the hunter, the
destroyer. If Thérèse seeks refuge from 'elle ne savait quel péril'
(p.31/40) and is terrified by 'cette puissance forcenée en moi et hors
de moi' (p.19/22), she is also the agent of that destructive force. She
imagines doing away with Bernard long before she administers
poison to him. Even as a child she recalls that 'quoi que prétendissent
mes maîtresses, je souffrais, je faisais souffrir. Je jouissais du mal
que je causais et de celui qui me venait de mes amies' (p.22/26). She
symbolically murders Jean Azévédo in a manner reminiscent of
witchcraft, stabbing his photograph with a pin and flushing it down
the lavatory; she tortures Anne mentally, trying to convince her that
happiness does not exist; she twice comes close to killing herself;
and she twice imagines herself committing arson, once just before
the 'grand incendie de Mano' when the desire gives way to thoughts
of murder, and once before Bernard returns in Chapter XII
(p.111/159). She is herself compared to a forest fire that creeps like a
snake: 'Au plus épais d'une famille, elle allait couver, pareille à un
feu sournois qui rampe sous la brande, embrase un pin, puis l'autre,
puis de proche en proche crée une forêt de torches' (p.33/43; cf.
p.32/42, 'ce reptile dans son sein'). This is something much more
sinister than mere revolt against the restrictions of family and
society. One of the models that is being proposed for Thérèse is that
of someone who has a vocation of destruction.

    The two models of victim and destroyer are both related to a
third, that of Thérèse as a body. In the opening pages of the novel,

her father and the lawyer are said to be 'gênés par ce corps de femme qui les séparait' (p.10/9). While she is intensely aware of Anne's body, she has a poor self-image where her own body is concerned. The 'femme ailée' discerned by Anne in the shapes of the clouds deteriorates into 'une étrange bête étendue' (p.28/35). During her honeymoon, when Anne's letter makes her aware of her own lack of fulfilment, she is described no longer as Bernard's wife, but as 'un être inconnu de lui, une créature étrangère et sans nom' (p.38/51): she has become an anonymous body. In so far as that body is female, she is a prey to the sexual demands of the male, but she sees herself as neuter (as she does other people: see *36*, p.28), and indeed inanimate: either as the trough in which the pig rootles for food, or as a lifeless corpse thrown up on a beach (pp. 35-36/46-47). She later distances herself from her body, seeing it as 'une vapeur suspendue en dehors d'elle' (p.79/109); she then tries to create an alternative body which would be able to make contact with other 'corps indistincts', but soon gives up the attempt: 'la pensée de Thérèse se détachait du corps inconnu qu'elle avait suscité pour sa joie' (p.107/152). In the final chapter she imagines herself running away through the Landes and collapsing on the sand where the crows, ants and dogs would make short work of her body (pp.125, 127/180, 183). It seems that her destructive urge is directed towards her own body. That may be a punishment for her presumed responsibility for her mother's death (see *39*, p.142), or an expression of her rejection of the physical aspect of human existence (she also wishes that her child would never have a physical existence, 'que cette créature inconnue ... ne se manifestât jamais', p.54/73), or else an outworking of some more mysterious force.

The exploration of the world of Thérèse does not produce any simple explanations of her character or actions in terms of her environment, her family background, spiritual forces, or other conditioning factors. 'Ces régions indéterminées où Thérèse a vécu, a souffert' (p.20/24) are characterized rather by shifting point of view, fluidity of time, fluctuation of mood, and plurality (of models and environments proposed by the text). The text is a structured whole, however, and a consideration of its structures will help us to form a more coherent overall view of the world of Thérèse.

5. Interpretations

Structures

Several structural approaches to *Thérèse Desqueyroux* have been tried. They may be subdivided into those which have a broad focus and those which have a narrow one. A broad structural approach is one that looks at the shape of the whole text and identifies the most important divisions, while a narrow one will concentrate on 'keys' and patterns within the text.

Sartre claimed that *La Fin de la nuit* had the structure of a play: 'Tout le roman tient en quatre scènes qui se terminent chacune par une "catastrophe" et dont chacune est exactement préparée comme dans une tragédie' (*42*, p.55). *Thérèse Desqueyroux*, for all its affinities with Racine's plays, is less obviously dramatic in structure. It seems to fall naturally into two parts rather than four: the first and last chapters, while in some sense acting as introduction and 'envoi' respectively, are none the less well integrated into the overall binary structure. The first part is constituted by the account of the journey to Argelouse, lasting one evening in autumn, during which Thérèse recalls episodes from her past. The second part is constituted by the account of the rest of the autumn and the following winter, at the end of which she goes to Paris. The division between these two parts is not entirely clear, however. Should Chapters IX and X be seen as belonging to the first part, in that they continue and conclude the account of the first evening and night, or to the second, in that Thérèse's attempts to reconstruct the past for Bernard's benefit and her own are now over, and the linear narrative of her imprisonment at Argelouse has begun? André Joubert takes the second option. For him the novel has a straightforward 'structure en étau'. Thérèse is caught in a vice-like grip: 'entre le poids du passé et celui des jours de confinement à Argelouse, Thérèse se trouve écrasée sans recours visibles' (*26*, p.19). The central point is her arrival at Argelouse at the beginning of Chapter IX. Until then she has been oppressed by the need to justify herself to Bernard, and thereafter she will face a different kind of oppression, imprisonment by the family. The first and last chapters provide a complementary frame, each describing an experience of liberation which turns out to be empty: 'Entre ces deux fausses libérations, une double oppression pèse sur Thérèse dans le roman' (*26*, p.18). Bernard Swift prefers the first option. The expected climaxes (the explanation of the crime and the confession to Bernard) having failed to materialize, Thérèse's destiny only catches up with her at the very end of the night that has lasted since the first chapter. The suicide attempt, with its aspect of ritual purging, provides an emotionally, aesthetically and structurally satisfying end to the long first section. It is a 'moment of intensity', when we are most acutely aware of 'the *fact* of Thérèse ... her existence as a static character' (*50*, pp.34, 37). The final two paragraphs of Chapter X then initiate an entirely new temporal structure.

But perhaps there is no need to identify a single turning-point in the novel. After all, even the suicide attempt is only a pseudo-climax, since it is forestalled by the discovery of Clara's death. It might be better to see Chapters IX and X as constituting a section in their own right. They are certainly given a remarkable unity, not only of time and place, but of theme, which might be summed up as 'clarity and the lack of it'. By the beginning of Chapter IX, Thérèse's attempts to 'voir clair' (p.22/27), to see clearly enough to explain her feelings and actions to Bernard, have failed. She arrives at Saint-Clair, whose name, insistently repeated throughout the preceding pages, now seems ironically mocking. Before she reaches Argelouse she is met by 'Monsieur et Mlle Clara' (p.87/121): the announcement is put into the mouth of Balion so that Bernard's name is not mentioned, and that of Clara, meaning the same as 'clair', is given prominence (see *23*, *24*, *32*). Clara immediately sits down between Thérèse and Bernard and chatters away, preventing any communication. The text thus offers an ironical preparation for the confrontation between Thérèse and Bernard, in which there is clarity in one sense — Bernard spells out the family's decision in terms that she cannot mistake — but no proper communication. The end of the chapter, however, introduces a more positive note. Clara's attempt to intervene may be frustrated by Bernard, but she does not give up: 'Elle demeure couchée sur son lit, les yeux ouverts' (p.95/134). Then, if Chapter X opens with Thérèse 'assise dans le noir', nevertheless 'des tisons vivaient encore sous la cendre' (p.96/135), and soon a clearer light returns. As she goes upstairs, 'A mesure qu'elle monte, elle y voit plus clair à cause de l'aube qui, là-haut, éclaire les vitres' (p.97/137). Her thoughts about suicide are tempered by the question: 'Comment renoncer à tant de lumière?' (p.99/139). When she is about to drink the poison, it is Clara who effectively prevents her (Balionte having discovered her body). Clarity, light, life: these may not be strongly present, but they are sufficient to keep a faint hope alive. At the end of the chapter Thérèse accepts a limited existence and a limited vision: 'vivre, mais comme un cadavre entre les mains de ceux qui la haïssent. N'essayer de rien voir au-delà' (p.100/141). The final image is an ambiguous one. Hemmed in at church by her family and the rest of the congregation, 'cela seulement lui est ouvert, comme l'arène au taureau qui sort de la nuit: cet espace vide, où, entre deux enfants, un homme déguisé est debout, chuchotant, les bras un peu écartés' (p.100/142). At least the bull is coming out of the darkness into the light, even if that light will bring death.[14] The priest may not be offering what Thérèse wants, but at least he symbolizes something radically different from the oppressive family. The last word, 'écartés', looks forward to Chapter XII, when 'il lui semblait que les pins s'écartaient' (p.118/168). In this middle section, then, the hope of clarity and openness is seemingly destroyed, only to be resurrected, albeit in a tentative fashion, by the end.

---

[14] In an interview in 1952, Mauriac gave a positive interpretation of that image. He said that he had always been particularly interested in people who were cut off on all sides, 'sauf du côté de Dieu, sauf du côté de l'Infini; exactement comme le taureau qui, dans le tauril, est obligé de passer par les couloirs sombres et ténébreux pour aboutir à l'arène et à l'épée' (5, p.219).

The boundaries of the sections are thus not clearly defined, as in the case of the 'scènes' of *La Fin de la nuit*, and there are no 'catastrophes', only pseudo-climaxes. There is more of a sense of ebb and flow than of forward movement. If Thérèse is seen essentially as a static character, it may be more appropriate to analyse the structure of the text in cyclical rather than linear terms. Marie-Françoise Canérot, for instance, claims that: 'l'héroïne vit trois fois le même cycle: angoisse diffuse, pacte avec la mort, espoir fallacieux de libération' (*11*, p.87). What underlying movement there is may be provided less by Thérèse herself than by the cycle of the seasons, which takes her through from autumn to spring.[15] Luisa Borella suggests a more complex musical model: three movements, each with its own brief introduction, and each punctuated by elements which may be at variance with the dominant tonality (see *10*).

Among those who have favoured a narrower structural approach is Alexander Fischler. He has pointed to the presence in the very first paragraph of the novel of a 'thematic key', defined as 'a statement that, as the result of semantic ambiguity, produces a number of themes interacting to the very end and seeming to offer a key to the entire structure' (*21*, p.377). Such keys, he claims, 'hold the novel together far more than the traditional plot'. The thematic key he identifies in *Thérèse Desqueyroux* is the expression 'non-lieu'. It is ostensibly a legal term with a very specific meaning: in the opinion of an examining magistrate there are no grounds for bringing a case. In Fischler's view, however, it expands and evolves to produce the whole text: a more ambitious claim than that of Marc Quaghebeur, who sees Thérèse's 'non-lieu' in terms of a 'mauvaise articulation avec ce que le psychanalyste entend par réel' (*39*, p.135). Thérèse finds that she cannot 'isolate the ground that fostered evil, or ... the ground on which there was an untainted innocence'. She comes to recognize that there is no place in the world 'où elle aurait pu s'épanouir' (p.87/121), 'no firm ground to determine her individ-

---

[15] John Flower notes that in *Thérèse Desqueyroux* Mauriac uses a motif, that of imprisonment, 'which is quite independent of any cyclic natural pattern and which is so dominant in fact that it causes the latter rather to be overlooked' (*22*, p.73).

uality'; yet in practice 'her only means of self-determination and self-
assertion is by reference to specific *lieux* ... and the people and
things within them', and she is unable to make her *non-lieu* absolute
by choosing death. Fischler concludes that she is condemned to
inhabit 'the world of the *non-lieu*, not only because it suspends
verdict on her, but because it offers no basis of judgment even to
those who would pass it on themselves' (*21*, p.382).

Fischler and Quaghebeur are not the only critics to see the
notion of *non-lieu* as a key to the novel. Maurice Maucuer extends it
to the whole 'cycle de Thérèse Desqueyroux' and to *Le Nœud de
vipères* as well: 'Thérèse, Louis, cherchent en vain leur lieu; mais
leurs actes eux-mêmes paraissent condamnés à ne jamais avoir lieu'
(*33*, p.219). Arthur Holmberg expresses the same idea in terms of the
moi. While Thérèse is fighting to 'protéger son moi individuel contre
la puissante mécanique familiale', her tragedy is that she does not
really have a *moi*. She is thus unable to transcend it and is
condemned to instability, torn between 'le désir de s'individualiser et
le désir de se perdre — dans le suicide ou dans une sorte de
symbiose' (*25*, p.130). Philip Solomon (see *48*) links *moi* and *lieu* by
appealing to the symbolic landscape of the novel. For him, Thérèse's
symbolic domain is the marsh of La Téchoueyre: 'she is mired in her
own indecisiveness', caught between refusal to accept the constraints
of life in Argelouse (the forest) and her inability to forsake Bernard
and seek freedom (symbolized by the ocean). Even in Paris a
metaphorical swampland awaits her.

Jean Touzot has also studied structure in terms of image and
symbol. One of his conclusions is that the structural centre of
Thérèse Desqueyroux is not the 'middle section' (Chapters IX and X)
at all, but Thérèse's marriage at the beginning of Chapter IV. For
Touzot, this novel is a remarkable example of the use of a technique
which he calls demarcation, whereby pairs of images mark out or
delimit 'les plans du récit', drawing attention to key episodes,
indicating shifts of time or place, and so on. He points out four pairs
of images in *Thérèse Desqueyroux* around which the whole novel is
organized: the pines which imprison and then release Thérèse (pp.12
& 118/12 & 168), the flock of sheep returning home (pp.29 & 65/37

& 90), the forest fire (pp.33 & 111/43 & 159), and the 'flot humain'
(pp.120-21 & 125/172-74 & 180). The middle two pairs both move
from a positive to a negative image; the first, which embraces them,
moves in the opposite direction; but that note of optimism is
immediately countered by the final pair which is duplicated,
emphasizing the destructive nature of the 'fleuve de boue'. This
'retour obsédant des symétries enveloppantes' has the effect of
emphasizing Thérèse's 'captivité toujours recommencée', while also
highlighting a particular moment: 'Centre des cercles démarcatifs et
centre de gravité du roman, le mariage renvoie constamment Thérèse
à un avant et à un après' (*54*, p.165).

     In fact the marriage itself is played down in the text: it is yet
another pseudo-climax, and the 'après' is not significantly different
from the 'avant' in terms of Thérèse's fundamental situation. Even
her change of name, from Larroque to Desqueyroux, is illusory. In
Mauriac's early drafts of the novel the names were interchangeable,
and in any case they have the same meaning. Desqueyroux is
ultimately derived from *caire*, a rock (see *24*, p.209: although
Touzot (*54*, pp.26, 319) appeals to popular etymology to suggest that
it is linked with *carrefour*).

     Analyses of structure seem to indicate that the potentially
decisive moments are not realized, and that Thérèse's existence is
characterized by ebb and flow rather than by any definite progres-
sion. What, then, are we to make of the hints of a possible religious
solution, in the Foreword and elsewhere in the text?

Religion and Crisis

Fernand Drijkoningen is quite clear that the text does not support
Mauriac's presumed didactic intentions, indeed that it works against
them: 'le romancier problématise l'idéologie chrétienne de Mauriac,
que celui-ci n'a pas su ni voulu dépasser' (*18*, p.67; cf. *41*). Are the
references to religious ideas, symbols and practice consistent with
the impression that is given of the world of Thérèse, on the one
hand, and with the spirit of the Foreword on the other?

Religious allusions in the text are few in comparison with many of Mauriac's other novels. Given the social setting, the references to the place of the church in the life of the community are plausible. Thérèse is married in church, and after her return to Argelouse after the *non-lieu* decision she is expected to attend Mass with her family in order to show that there is nothing the matter. Bernard fulfils his duty as a major local landowner by taking part in the Corpus Christi procession ('la Fête-Dieu', p.79/110). His mother sees saintliness in entirely secular and practical terms: Bernard is 'un saint' (p.92/129), and the anticlerical Jérôme Larroque is 'un saint laïque' (p.30/39). Bernard wishes that Thérèse believed in God because it would make her behave better: 'la peur est le commencement de la sagesse' (p.94/132). Thérèse herself, with the influence of her father and her *lycée* education, has little time for religion, which is simply part of the whole repressive environment against which she rebels: 'Les dames du Sacré-Cœur interposaient mille voiles entre le réel et leurs petites filles. Thérèse les méprisait de confondre vertu et ignorance' (p.22/27). At her wedding, the image of the 'étroite église de Saint-Clair où le caquetage des dames couvrait l'harmonium à bout de souffle et où leurs odeurs triomphaient de l'encens' (p.33/43) is quickly followed by that of the cage, and the 'fracas de la lourde porte refermée', so strongly emphasized in the film,[16] completes the identification. In her solitude and frustration, however, it is not surprising that Thérèse should later begin to look to religion for help. The priest intrigues her: 'Quel réconfort puisait-il dans ces rites quotidiens?' (p.77/106); 'à qui parlait-il avec cet air de douleur?' (p.79/110). Those questions come either side of the birth of Marie, which Thérèse had wished would never happen: 'elle aurait voulu connaître un Dieu pour obtenir de lui que cette créature inconnue, toute mêlée encore à ses entrailles, ne se manifestât jamais' (p.54/73). Indeed it seems that Thérèse's interest in God is associated with the anxieties of birth and

---

16 Claude Mauriac comments that Georges Franju, 'aussi fermé au surnaturel que Mauriac en était proche', played down the religious significance of the text in his film (see his 'Postface' to the 1988 Livre de poche edition, p.189; cf. *34*, p.150).

death. God is later asked, if He exists, to save her from suicide, or
failing that, to 'accueillir avec amour ce monstre, sa créature'
(p.99/140). When the immediate danger is past Thérèse loses
interest, although attendance at Mass offers her 'quelque relâche'
from her situation as a social pariah (p.102/145) — until Bernard
stops her going. Thinking back to her conversations with Jean
Azévédo in which religious ideas played a large part, she comments:
'Je crois bien que je vomirais aujourd'hui ce ragoût' (p.64/88).
Religion is thus either part of the social fabric, or a temporary form
of escapism, or a source of psychological support in times of
anxiety. It offers no real solution. Writing about *Thérèse Desqueyroux*, Mauriac's biographer Jean Lacouture claimed that: 'Aucun de
ses livres n'est aussi froidement déserté par la foi, aussi lourd de
l'absence de Dieu' (*28*, p.217). Mauriac himself admitted that:
'Thérèse, c'est moi désespéré' (*5*, p.88). Religion may be present, but
not in the sense of active divine grace. Thérèse would appear to be
no better off than the pagan Phèdre.

Such a view does not, however, do full justice to the text.
Religion does have more to offer, and Thérèse is more open than has
just been suggested. In the first place, Christianity is not strictly
identified with the repressive social environment. At the Corpus
Christi procession, Thérèse despises Bernard precisely because of
the sharp contrast between his purely formal participation and the
radical challenge posed to society by the ceremony. Most of the
inhabitants of Saint-Clair at least recognize that challenge: they hide
away, 'comme si c'eût été un lion, et non un agneau, qu'on avait
lâché dans les rues' (p.79/110). Bernard, on the other hand, is totally
indifferent. His mind and his physical gestures are 'à la voie'
(p.126/181), and the 'vie de l'esprit' (p.65/89) which Jean Azévédo
exalted is foreign to him. When Thérèse, encouraged by Jean, starts
to take an interest in the young priest, she discovers not merely a
fellow-inhabitant of the desert and a fellow-intellectual, but a sacra-
mental pointer to an alternative reality:

> sans autre témoin que l'enfant de chœur, il murmurait
> des paroles, courbé sur un morceau de pain.
>
> (pp.77/106-07)
>
> Thérèse dévisagea le curé, qui avançait les yeux
> presque fermés, portant des deux mains cette chose
> étrange. Ses lèvres remuaient: à qui parlait-il avec cet air
> de douleur? (p.79/110)
>
> elle revoit ... l'homme solitaire écrasé sous une chape
> d'or, et cette chose qu'il porte des deux mains, et ces
> lèvres qui remuent, et cet air de douleur ... (p.99/140)
>
> cet espace vide, où, entre deux enfants, un homme
> déguisé est debout, chuchotant, les bras un peu écartés.
>
> (p.100/142)

The priest is the antithesis of human society. He is not a dominating male but 'un homme déguisé', himself oppressed and suffering: he is not in solidarity with society but cut off from it, alone or accompanied only by children, and in communion with an unseen presence; his words are neither predictable nor oppressive but mysterious; his centre of attention is not food or property but 'cette chose étrange', a monstrance containing bread that is more than bread. That mysterious alternative reality continues to attract Thérèse even after she has attained the immediate goal of liberation in Paris, where she still dreams of 'toute une vie de méditation, de perfectionnement, dans le silence d'Argelouse: l'aventure intérieure, la recherche de Dieu...' (p.122/174). Roger Bichelberger has suggested that in Mauriac's novels, revolt against society and indeed against social forms of religion has a positive aspect to it, in that it is 'la première étape de la révolte essentielle qui est une révolte vers' (8, p.58). Thérèse's revolt, springing from inside herself as well as from her confrontation with society, is not just a 'révolte contre' but also, at least potentially, a 'révolte vers, un acquiescement à l'Amour qui est, comme on sait, l'autre nom de Dieu'.

But how far does she get? Is she not merely straining towards *any* symbol of freedom: the wind in the trees outside her window, the ocean, Paris, God? Even marriage was ironically seen in terms of salvation at the time: 'Elle se sauvait' (p.31/40). The primary meaning of 'se sauver' here is 'escape, run away'; the secondary meaning is indeed largely ironical; but the very choice of the verb at least keeps the possibility of a religious salvation open, and it would be wrong to assert that the text itself denies that possibility. Several indications in the middle section of the novel serve to support it. Thérèse comes to the point of praying, and there is a clear development from 'elle aurait voulu connaître un Dieu pour obtenir de lui ... ' (p.54/73) to 'S'il existe, cet Etre ... qu'Il détourne la main' and finally to 'puisse-t-Il, du moins, accueillir avec amour ce monstre, sa créature' (p.99/140).[17] Clara's death is presented as explainable in terms both of an answer to that prayer and of a sacrificial laying down of her life for Thérèse, although Mauriac is careful to note that: 'si on lui parlait d'une volonté particulière, elle hausserait les épaules' (p.100/141). Alastair Duncan (see *20*) associates these features with the shift from darkness to light that occurs in several successive paragraphs of Chapter X and with the final image of the priest, which symbolizes openness, to underline the permanence of hope, and a religious hope at that, in the midst of intense despair. Thérèse has not yet embraced that hope, but it is still there. Luisa Borella is even more positive. She takes the 'mort par amour' of Clara, Thérèse's deliverance from death, and her later experience of physical suffering at the end of Chapter XI (seen as her 'raison d'être au monde' and as the price of her recovery) as three indications of the existence of 'cette nappe de vie souterraine qui, désormais, alimentera la jeune femme' (*10*, p.222; cf. *9*, p.245).

There is no inconsistency here with the portrayal of the obscure world of Thérèse, whose dimensions include the spiritual and the mythical as well as the material and the social. The model of

---

[17] The 'puisqu'Il existe' of the older Livre de poche text, following the first edition, is not retained in that of the *Œuvres complètes* of 1950, or in the new Livre de poche edition of 1989. Strangely, the Pléiade edition, based on the 1950 text, does not even record it as a variant.

the sinner in need of salvation is as plausible as those of the social rebel or the tragic heroine.[18]

At the structural level, the cycle of the seasons is often given a spiritual significance by Mauriac, with the spring being associated with rebirth. The cycle of the liturgical calendar may also have a discreet role to play in this novel (see 24). In the first autumn of her married life Thérèse is introduced to mystical ideas by Jean Azévédo, and may thus be imitating her patron saint, Teresa of Avila, the great Spanish mystic (feast-day 15 October).[19] In the second autumn, when Clara is ill, Thérèse 'mit beaucoup de bonne volonté à la relayer auprès des pauvres gens d'Argelouse' (p.83/115), copying the simple good works of her other patron saint, Thérèse de l'Enfant Jésus (Thérèse de Lisieux, feast-day 3 October). The third autumn is that of the *non-lieu* decision: Thérèse is trying to establish her own identity, having thrown off those of her patron saints. In the course of Chapter XI she creates several imaginary personae for herself, ranging from the modern liberated Parisian woman to the saint who ironically heals an 'enfant d'Argelouse (un de ceux qui fuyaient à son approche)' (p.107/152) by the imposition of her nicotine-stained hand. There is no substance to these, however. In the Foreword Mauriac proposes an authentically new identity for her, involving a change of name, to Sainte Locuste (and thus the redemption of her destructive nature),[20] and a change of season, to the spring.

But this is only a proposal, alongside the other models put forward in the course of the text. Mauriac's hope is expressed in the past conditional: 'J'aurais voulu que la douleur, Thérèse, te livre à Dieu' (p.7/6). He has engaged with her closely, but ultimately he

---

[18] Thérèse can even be seen as the archetypal *femme fatale* (see Maurice Maucuer, 'Sainte Locuste', in 6), who may be identified as Eve, or possibly Lilith, to Bernard's Adam (p.44/60); or possibly as the destructive Earth-mother Cybele who mutilated and killed her beloved Attis and turned him into a pine-tree (Mauriac began writing his poem 'Le Sang d'Atys' shortly after completing *Thérèse Desqueyroux*).

[19] André Joubert suggests other possible parallels between Thérèse Desqueyroux and Teresa of Avila (see 26, pp.176-77).

[20] See Maucuer, 'Sainte Locuste', in 6.

respects her autonomy. He recognizes that her world is complex, and he will neither dictate her choices nor deny the spiritual dimension. When he peers into the future, it is not to limit her but to draw attention to the persistence of that complexity:

> Il y aurait des aubes de sa future vie, de cette inimaginable vie, des aubes si désertes qu'elle regretterait peut-être l'heure du réveil à Argelouse, l'unique clameur des coqs sans nombre. Elle se souviendra, dans les étés qui vont venir, des cigales du jour et des grillons de la nuit.
>
> (p.119/170)

Lying behind the text of *Thérèse Desqueyroux* is Mauriac's intense personal crisis. Identifying himself with Racine, he is experiencing 'ce réveil du sang chrétien ... aux abords de la quarantaine', but he is also painfully aware that 'notre révolte est d'autant plus furieuse que nous sentons plus résistante la chaîne qui nous lie au Dieu de notre enfance' (*4*, pp.100, 80). He can as yet grasp no solution, but he believes that 'Dieu ne peut exiger que je me détruise et c'est me détruire que d'étouffer l'œuvre que je porte' (*4*, p.80). Thérèse's struggle against *étouffement*, and her anguished exploration of her world, mirror the struggle of Mauriac's text, both written and lived, to find expression. 'Thérèse, c'est moi désespéré' means not that all hope has gone, but that hope cannot yet be firmly embraced (it is only fair to point out that what Mauriac actually said was: 'Si vous voulez, Thérèse Desqueyroux, c'est moi désespéré, mais je ne suis pas désespéré' (*5*, p.88), but that was a quarter of a century after the publication of the novel). As a text of crisis and exploration, *Thérèse Desqueyroux*, including the Foreword, is self-consistent.

6. Conclusion

'Pourquoi Thérèse Desqueyroux a-t-elle voulu empoisonner son mari? Ce point d'interrogation a beaucoup fait pour retenir au milieu de nous son ombre douloureuse' (2, p.849): so Mauriac noted in his essay *Le Romancier et ses personnages* in 1932. The reasons for Thérèse's crime cannot be fully analysed in terms of heredity or environment or other determining factors, and they are not much clearer at the end of the novel than they were earlier on. That is partly because of the indeterminate nature of Thérèse's character, and partly because of the way Mauriac writes. Michel Raimond comments that Mauriac's practice of 'esquisser des mouvements vers la psychologie profonde pour y renoncer aussitôt' leaves it uncertain whether he is yielding to a 'besoin de rapidité' or whether it is 'pour mieux sauvegarder l'efficacité esthétique'. He seems to accept the second explanation in the end, suggesting that *Thérèse Desqueyroux* points the way forward to novels in which 'le langage n'est plus que l'occasion d'une contestation de toute définition'.[21] Social, sexual and spiritual forces all have their part to play in making Thérèse the person she is, but so do more literary considerations: mythologies of woman, metaphor, rhetoric. Jean Touzot sees the novel as a prime example of syllepsis, a rhetorical figure in which the proper sense of a word coexists with its figurative use. The three cases he cites are those of *étouffement*, *poison* and *écarter* or *effacer* (see *53*, pp.57-58). Thérèse is implicated in all three, as victim in the first and third, and as aggressor in the second and third. Critics who have seen Mauriac's fiction as merely a continuation of the 'héritage du roman psychologico-naturaliste du XIXe siècle' are doing him an

---

[21] Michel Raimond, *La Crise du roman* (Paris, Corti, 1967), pp.457, 460.

injustice.[22] *Thérèse Desqueyroux* is a truly modern text, full of shifting patterns, and quite unlike the analytical and didactic tradition to which such critics would assimilate it.

The choice of *Thérèse Desqueyroux*, by a panel presided over by Colette in 1950, as one of the best dozen novels of the first half of the century, probably owed more to the intensity of Mauriac's imagery and to the compelling power of the figure of Thérèse herself than to the aesthetic modernity of the text or even to its value as social satire. The imagery arises naturally out of the geographical and social setting, and effectively replaces it with an imaginary universe. Thus Argelouse is three times said to be ten kilometres from Saint-Clair, even though in real life the distance from Saint-Symphorien to Jouanhaut is only about five kilometres, because it is important to emphasize that 'Argelouse est réellement une extrémité de la terre' (p.24/29). The imaginary universe is largely dark, and full of restrictive straight lines: roads, paths, railway lines, walls, bars, rain, pine trees. This sense of intensity and restriction imprints itself on the reader's mind more strongly than the actual details of Thérèse's history. Cecil Jenkins accepts that 'the validity of this "problem-novel" is in the end the validity of poetry' (Jenkins, p.42). Within that poetic climate lies the problem of Thérèse herself. For Mauriac, writing in 1952, she is 'l'être qui échappe à tout jugement, et d'abord au sien propre, terriblement libre à chaque instant, et regardant sa figure éternelle se dessiner au moindre geste qu'elle hasarde' ('Vue sur mes romans', in *6*, p.167), the epitome of the tension between destiny and free will. She is a question-mark, mercifully free of 'la complaisance et la satisfaction' (*2*, p.852). Bernard Swift draws attention to the danger of trying to pin her down, to reduce her to 'une image stéréotypée' (*51*, p.221). Interrogation, then, is perhaps the key to *Thérèse Desqueyroux* (see *40*): not merely about the character and actions of a woman called Thérèse Desqueyroux, but about Mauriac's own crisis, about psychology and destiny more generally, about salvation, and about

---

[22] Gaëtan Picon, *Panorama de la nouvelle littérature française* (Paris, Gallimard, 1976), p.35.

the nature of a literary text. *Thérèse Desqueyroux* seems more richly interrogative today than when it was written.

Bibliography

The new Livre de poche edition by Jean Touzot includes an introduction, a section entitled 'Approches de l'œuvre', and a brief bibliography, all of which will be found helpful. There are older student editions by Jean-Marie Pény (Livre de poche Université) and André Lanly (Bordas: Univers des lettres). The best edition for English readers remains that by Cecil Jenkins (University of London Press, 1964).

1. François Mauriac, *Œuvres romanesques et théâtrales complètes*, I (Paris, Gallimard: Bibliothèque de la Pléiade, 1978). This excellent critical edition, by Jacques Petit, is indispensable. The first volume includes *Le Désert de l'amour*, *Coups de couteau* and the Preface to Volume II of the *Œuvres complètes* (Fayard) which covers *Thérèse Desqueyroux* and its sequels.

2. ——, *Œuvres romanesques et théâtrales complètes*, II (Paris, Gallimard: Bibliothèque de la Pléiade, 1979). Includes *Conscience, instinct divin*, *Thérèse Desqueyroux*, *La Province* and *Le Roman*.

3. ——, *Œuvres romanesques et théâtrales complètes*, III (Paris, Gallimard: Bibliothèque de la Pléiade, 1981). Includes *Thérèse chez le docteur*, *Thérèse à l'hôtel* and *La Fin de la nuit*.

4. ——, *Œuvres complètes*, VIII (Paris, Fayard: Bibliothèque Bernard Grasset, 1952). Includes *La Vie de Jean Racine*.

5. ——, *Souvenirs retrouvés: entretiens avec Jean Amrouche* (Paris, Fayard/Institut National de l'Audiovisuel, 1981): pp.205-33 are largely devoted to *Thérèse Desqueyroux*.

6. *François Mauriac* (Paris, Les Editions de l'Herne: *Les Cahiers de l'Herne*, 48, 1985). Contains a wide range of *inédits* and critical articles, in particular two on *Thérèse Desqueyroux* by Bernard Chochon and Maurice Maucuer.

7. *François Mauriac. Visions and Reappraisals*, edited by John E. Flower and Bernard C. Swift (Oxford, New York, Munich: Berg, 1989). A stimulating collection of articles by English-speaking scholars, including one specifically on *Thérèse Desqueyroux* by William Kidd.

There have been several special numbers of reviews devoted to Mauriac in connection with the centenary of his birth, notably the *Australian Journal of French Studies*, 22, 2 (1985) and *La Revue des deux mondes*, February 1986. Individual articles in these special numbers are listed below, as are articles in the three specialist series devoted to Mauriac: the *Cahiers François Mauriac* (Paris, Grasset), the *Travaux du Centre d'Etudes et de Recherches sur François Mauriac* (Bordeaux, Presses Universitaires de Bordeaux), and the series *François Mauriac* of the *Revue des lettres modernes*.

8. Bichelberger, Roger, 'La Révolte dans les romans de François Mauriac', *Travaux du Centre ...*, 23 (1988), 51-61. A condensed version of the same author's *Rencontre avec Mauriac* (Paris, Editions de l'Ecole, 1973).

9. Borella, Luisa, *Approche de Thérèse Desqueyroux* (Parma, Casanova, 1976). A useful workbook designed for Italian students reading a French novel for the first time. Contains a perceptive 'Essai sur *Thérèse Desqueyroux*'.

10. ———, 'Aspects du discours féminin chez Mauriac romancier', *Cahiers François Mauriac*, 13 (1986), 216-26. On *Thérèse Desqueyroux*.

11. Canérot, Marie-Françoise, *Mauriac après 1930: le roman dénoué* (Paris, SEDES, 1985). Some illuminating references to *Thérèse Desqueyroux*, despite the title.

12. ———, 'Province, terre d'inspiration', *La Revue des deux mondes* (February 1986), 340-53.

13. Chochon, Bernard, *François Mauriac ou la passion de la terre* (Paris, Minard: *Archives des lettres modernes*, 140, 1972).

14. ———, 'Signes et figures dans *Thérèse Desqueyroux*', *La Revue des lettres modernes*, 707-709 (*François Mauriac 4: Mauriac romancier*, 1984), 11-33.

15. Cormeau, Nelly, *L'Art de François Mauriac* (Paris, Grasset, 1951). Old and rather uncritical, but still worth reading.

16. Croc, Paul, 'Mauriac et la technique du point de vue', *Cahiers François Mauriac*, 2 (1975), 26-42.

17. Delbouille, Paul, 'Le Double Voyage de Thérèse Desqueyroux', *Cahiers d'analyse textuelle*, 7 (1965), 7-24.

18. Drijkoningen, Fernand, 'Lire autrement *Thérèse Desqueyroux*', *Rapports - Het Franse Boek*, 54 (1984), 63-68.

19. Dubois-Salem, Anne-Marie, 'Une Femme affranchie: Thérèse Desqueyroux', *Travaux du Centre ...*, 16 (1984), 7-31.

20. Duncan, Alastair B., 'Despair and Hope in *Thérèse Desqueyroux*', *Modern Languages*, 63 (September 1982), 168-72.

21. Fischler, Alexander, 'Thematic Keys in François Mauriac's *Thérèse Desqueyroux* and *Le Nœud de vipères*', *Modern Language Quarterly*, 40 (1979), 376-89.

22. Flower, J.E., *Intention and Achievement. An Essay on the Novels of François Mauriac* (Oxford, Clarendon Press, 1969). An important study of Mauriac as a Catholic novelist.

23. ———, 'Tunnels in *Thérèse Desqueyroux*', *Australian Journal of French Studies*, 22 (1985), 126-37.

24. Garfitt, J.S.T., 'Clés pour *Thérèse Desqueyroux*: onomastique et calendrier liturgique', in *Présence de François Mauriac* (Bordeaux, Presses Universitaires de Bordeaux, 1986), 209-15. This volume contains the papers read at the Colloque du Centenaire in 1985.

25. Holmberg, Arthur, 'Thérèse Desqueyroux: l'impossibilité du moi', *Cahiers François Mauriac*, 13 (1986), 125-37.

26. Joubert, André J., *François Mauriac et Thérèse Desqueyroux* (Paris, Nizet, 1982). The only full-length study of the novel, but with a surprisingly thin bibliography.

27. Lacour, Guy, 'Expérience pédagogique sur *Thérèse Desqueyroux* en formation continue', *Travaux du Centre ...*, 23 (1988), 115-25. The same number contains another account of an 'expérience pédagogique', this time in the *classe de troisième*, and based on several novels by Mauriac (including *Thérèse Desqueyroux*).

28. Lacouture, Jean, *François Mauriac* (Paris, Editions du Seuil, 1980). The best biography of Mauriac, with a chapter entitled 'Thérèse et moi'.

29. Lane, Brigitte, '"Pseudo-mères" et "pseudo-épouses": bourreaux et victimes dans quatre romans de François Mauriac', *Cahiers François Mauriac*, 13 (1986), 93-104.

30. Martin du Gard, Roger, 'Lettre à François Mauriac (1927)', *La Revue des deux mondes* (February 1986), 359-60.

31. Maucuer, Maurice, *Thérèse Desqueyroux, Mauriac* (Paris, Hatier: Coll. Profil d'une œuvre, 1970). A useful guide for students.

32. ———, 'La Nuit dans les romans de François Mauriac', *Australian Journal of French Studies*, 22 (1985), 159-66.

33. ———, 'Lieu et non-lieu dans le cycle de *Thérèse Desqueyroux* et dans *Le Nœud de vipères*', *Cahiers François Mauriac*, 14 (1987), 213-24.

34. Milner, Max, 'Du roman au cinéma, commentaires sur l'adaptation cinématographique de *Thérèse Desqueyroux* par Georges Franju', *Cahiers François Mauriac*, 2 (1975), 148-59.

35. Monférier, Jacques, 'Thérèse Desqueyroux, Phèdre et le destin', *La Revue des lettres modernes*, 516-22 (*François Mauriac 2: François Mauriac et la grâce*, 1977), 109-18.

36. Mounin, Georges, 'Structure, fonction, pertinence: à propos de *Thérèse Desqueyroux*', *La Linguistique*, 10 (1974), 21-32. A statistical approach to the text.

37. Niel, André, *L'Analyse structurale des textes: littérature, presse, publicité* (Paris, Mame, 1973). Contains two long chapters devoted to a psycho-structural analysis of *Thérèse Desqueyroux*, with the apparent

purpose of helping the reader to come to terms with the 'ambiguïté douloureuse de la conscience moderne'.

38. Petit, Pierre, *'Thérèse Desqueyroux*: mythe solaire et imagerie conflictuelle', *Travaux du Centre* ..., 16 (1984), 33-39.

39. Quaghebeur, Marc, *'Thérèse Desqueyroux'*, *Cahiers François Mauriac*, 2 (1975), 133-47. A psychoanalytical approach.

40. Raimond, Michel, 'Mauriac et le discours psychologique', *Cahiers François Mauriac*, 2 (1975), 187-97. Cf. the chapter entitled 'La Psychologie de l'inconscient et ses problèmes' in his *La Crise du roman* (Paris, Corti, 1967).

41. Reid, James H., 'Mauriac, the Ambivalent Author of Absence', *Studies in Twentieth Century Literature*, 11 (Spring 1987), 167-88. On first- and third-person narrative in *Thérèse Desqueyroux* and *Le Nœud de vipères*.

42. Sartre, Jean-Paul, 'M. François Mauriac et la liberté', in *Situations*, I (Paris, Gallimard, 1947), 36-57. Sartre's classic attack on Mauriac as a novelist ('Dieu n'est pas un artiste; M. Mauriac non plus').

43. Schwarzenbach, James, *François Mauriac, der Dichter zwiespältigen Lebens* (Cologne, Benziger, 1938). Devotes a substantial chapter to *Thérèse Desqueyroux*.

44. Scott, Malcolm, *Mauriac, the Politics of a Novelist* (Edinburgh, Scottish Academic Press, 1980). Good on the moral/artistic dilemma of *Thérèse Desqueyroux*.

45. Séailles, André, *Mauriac* (Paris, Bordas: Coll. Présence littéraire, 1972). Good general study of Mauriac's writings.

46. ——, 'Les Techniques narratives dans le cycle de *Thérèse Desqueyroux'*, *Cahiers de l'Association Internationale des Etudes Françaises*, 36 (1984), 53-68.

47. Shillony, Helena, 'La Femme intellectuelle dans les romans de Mauriac', *Cahiers François Mauriac*, 13 (1986), 115-24.

48. Solomon, Philip H., 'Symbolic Landscape and the Quest for Self in François Mauriac's *Thérèse Desqueyroux'*, *Forum for Modern Language Studies*, 22 (1986), 16-21.

49. Sutton, Geneviève, 'Phèdre et Thérèse Desqueyroux: une communauté de destin', *French Review*, 43 (1970), 559-70.

50. Swift, Bernard C., 'Structure and Meaning in *Thérèse Desqueyroux'*, *Wascana Review*, 5 (1970), 33-44.

51. ——, 'Jeunesse et destin chez *Thérèse Desqueyroux*: l'énigme du passé', *Cahiers François Mauriac*, 11 (1984), 215-27.

52. Tolton, C.D.E., 'The *Revirement*: a Structural Key to the Novels of François Mauriac', *Australian Journal of French Studies*, 12 (1975), 105-13.

53. Touzot, Jean, *François Mauriac, une configuration romanesque: profil rhétorique et stylistique* (Paris, Minard: *Archives des lettres modernes*, 218, 1985). Sees *Thérèse Desqueyroux* as the novel of syllepsis.

54. ——, *La Planète Mauriac. Figure d'analogie et roman* (Paris, Klincksieck, 1985).

CRITICAL GUIDES TO FRENCH TEXTS

edited by

Roger Little, Wolfgang van Emden, David Williams

CRITICAL GUIDES TO FRENCH TEXTS

edited by
Roger Little, Wolfgang van Emden, David Williams

1. **David Bellos.** Balzac: La Cousine Bette.
2. **Rosemarie Jones.** Camus: L'Etranger *and* La Chute.
3. **W.D Redfern.** Queneau: Zazie dans le métro.
4. **R.C. Knight.** Corneille: Horace.
5. **Christopher Todd.** Voltaire: Dictionnaire philosophique.
6. **J.P. Little.** Beckett: En attendant Godot *and* Fin de partie.
7. **Donald Adamson.** Balzac: Illusions perdues.
8. **David Coward.** Duras: Moderato cantabile.
9. **Michael Tilby.** Gide: Les Faux-Monnayeurs.
10. **Vivienne Mylne.** Diderot: La Religieuse.
11. **Elizabeth Fallaize.** Malraux: La Voie Royale.
12. **H.T Barnwell.** Molière: Le Malade imaginaire.
13. **Graham E. Rodmell.** Marivaux: Le Jeu de l'amour et du hasard *and* Les Fausses Confidences.
14. **Keith Wren.** Hugo: Hernani *and* Ruy Blas.
15. **Peter S. Noble.** Beroul's Tristan *and the* Folie de Berne.
16. **Paula Clifford.** Marie de France: Lais.
17. **David Coward.** Marivaux: La Vie de Marianne *and* Le Paysan parvenu.
18. **J.H. Broome.** Molière: L'Ecole des femmes *and* Le Misanthrope.
19. **B.G. Garnham.** Robbe-Grillet: Les Gommes *and* Le Voyeur.
20. **J.P. Short.** Racine: Phèdre.
21. **Robert Niklaus.** Beaumarchais: Le Mariage de Figaro.
22. **Anthony Cheal Pugh.** Simon: Histoire.
23. **Lucie Polak.** Chrétien de Troyes: Cligés.
24. **John Cruickshank.** Pascal: Pensées.
25. **Ceri Crossley.** Musset: Lorenzaccio.
26. **J.W. Scott.** Madame de Lafayette: La Princesse de Clèves.
27. **John Holyoake.** Montaigne: Essais.
28. **Peter Jimack.** Rousseau: Emile.
29. **Roger Little.** Rimbaud: Illuminations.

61. **Geoffrey N. Bromiley.** Thomas's Tristan *and the* Folie Tristan d'Oxford.
62. **R.J. Howells.** Rousseau: Julie ou la Nouvelle Héloise.
63. **George Evans.** Lesage: Crispin rival de son maître *and* Turcaret.
64. **Paul Reed.** Sartre: La Nausée.
65. **Roger McLure.** Sarraute: Le Planétarium.
66. **Denis Boak.** Sartre: Les Mots.
67. **Pamela M. Moores.** Vallès: L'Enfant.
68. **Simon Davies.** Laclos: Les Liaisons dangereuses.
69. **Keith Beaumont.** Jarry: Ubu Roi.
70. **G.J. Mallinson.** Molière: L'Avare.
71. **Susan Taylor-Horrex.** Verlaine: Fêtes galantes *and* Romances sans paroles.
72. **Malcolm Cook.** Lesage: Gil Blas.
74. **W.D. Howarth.** Corneille: Le Cid.
73. **Sheila Bell.** Sarraute: Portrait d'un inconnu *and* Vous les entendez?
75. **Peter Jimack.** Diderot: Supplément au Voyage de Bougainville.
76. **Christopher Lloyd.** Maupassant: Bel-Ami.
77. **David H. Walker.** Gide: Les Nourritures terrestres *and* La Symphonie pastorale
78. **Noël Peacock.** Molière: Les Femmes savantes.
79. **Jean H. Duffy.** Butor: La Modification.
80. **J.P. Little.** Genet: Les Nègres.
81. **John Campbell.** Racine: Britannicus.
82. **Malcolm Quainton.** D'Aubigné: Les Tragiques.
83. **Henry Phillips.** Racine: Mithidrate.
84. **S. Beynon John.** Saint-Exupéry: Vol de Nuit *and* Terre des hommes.
85. **John Trethewey.** Corneille: L'Illusion comique *and* Le Menteur.
86. **John Dunkley.** Beaumarchais: Le Barbier de Séville.
87. **Valerie Minogue.** Zola: L'Assommoir.
88. **Kathleen Hall.** Rabelais: Pantagruel and Gargantua.